A New Translation of Isaiah

Based on Ancient Scrolls and Texts

Translated and Edited By

Donald W. Parry

Foreword by Shon D. Hopkin

FAIR
2026

Published by FAIR
PO Box 491677, Redding, CA 96049
For permissions, academic inquiries, or bulk orders, contact:
dbeck@fairlatterdaysaints.org

Book Design, Typesetting, and Copyediting: Jared Riddick
Cover Image: The Great Isaiah Scroll (1QIsa[a]). Photograph by Ardon Bar Hama. Courtesy of The Israel Museum, Jerusalem. Public domain.

Publisher's Cataloging-in-Publication Data
Names: Parry, Donald W., author. | Hopkin, Shon D., author.
Title: A new translation of Isaiah : based on ancient scrolls and texts / Donald W. Parry.
Description: First edition. | Redding, CA : FAIR, 2026. | Includes bibliographical references.

Identifiers: LCCN 2026936145 (print) | ISBN 978-1-971818-01-6 (hardcover) | ISBN 978-1-971818-00-9 (paperback) | ISBN 978-1-971818-02-3 (ebook)

Subjects: LCSH: Bible. Isaiah--Criticism, interpretation, etc. | Bible. Old Testament--Language, style. | Hebrew language--Parallelism. | Bible--Study and teaching--Church of Jesus Christ of Latter-day Saints. | Book of Mormon--Relation to the Bible. | Dead Sea scrolls. | BISAC: RELIGION / Biblical Criticism & Interpretation / Old Testament. | RELIGION / Biblical Studies / Old Testament / Prophets. | RELIGION / Biblical Reference / Language Study. | RELIGION / Christianity / Church of Jesus Christ of Latter-day Saints (Mormon)

Classification: LCC BS1515.52 .P37 2026 (print) | LCC BS1515.52 (ebook) | DDC 224.106--dc23.

First edition: April 2026

Produced and published in the United States of America

Table of Contents

Acknowledgments

I express gratitude to Professor Shon D. Hopkin, a prominent Isaiah scholar and formerly the chair of Ancient Scripture, Brigham Young University, for writing the Foreword. Although Professor Hopkin is presently directing a significant program in Jerusalem, Israel, he authored the Foreword in spite of his time-pressed schedule.

Two well-known Isaiah scholars from Brigham Young University—Professors Shon D. Hopkin (mentioned above) and Terry Ball (formerly the Dean, now an emeritus professor)—carefully read the manuscript; I thank them for their kind support, words of encouragement, and insightful and invaluable comments. Both Professors Hopkin and Ball have provided me with direction as I approached Isaiah, including formatting into parallelisms, notes and comments, and the speakers of Isaiah. I also extend appreciation to two reviewers who served as "double-blind" reviewers/scholars for their many helpful comments and suggestions; their comments also served to improve the manuscript.

Several individuals helped me to polish and fine-tune this volume. I extend great appreciation to Jared Riddick, for creating the cover design, for copyediting, and for the interior design and typesetting. *A New Translation of Isaiah: Based on Ancient Scrolls and Texts* presented distinct challenges, chiefly because the approximately 1,100 parallelistic structures and the more than 100 chiastic structures required special attention. Jared helped me work through these challenges!

I appreciate the professionalism of editor Kim Sandoval, as she edited my manuscript and provided numerous improvements in style, grammar, and presentation. Over many years Kim has provided me with the highest level of professionalism and competence; as the saying goes, "behind every author is a brilliant editor."

Foreword

The Book of Isaiah is the "Great Barrier Reef" of scripture—vibrant, soul-deep, and occasionally daunting to those who swim its waters. For members of The Church of Jesus Christ of Latter-day Saints, the mandate to "search these things diligently" comes directly from the Savior. Yet, the beauty of Isaiah is often locked behind the complexities of ancient Hebrew nuance and the constraints of traditional English translations. Sitting in the classroom of Donald W. Parry is a transformative experience for any student seeking to unlock these complexities. Having had the privilege of studying Biblical Hebrew under his direction, I have seen firsthand how his scholarship is matched only by his devotion to the sacred text. His mentorship and generosity of spirit have blessed my subsequent career in too many instances to count.

Dr. Parry's work has long served as a bridge between the rigorous world of academic discovery and the spiritual needs of Latter-day Saints. This new translation represents the completion of a vital trilogy of works dedicated to the prophet. It builds upon the foundation laid by his comprehensive verse-by-verse commentary, *Understanding Isaiah* (1998), and his more recent introductory guide, *Search Diligently the Words of Isaiah* (2023). Together, these three works provide a unified toolkit, inviting every reader to search Isaiah's writings more deeply in order to "learn and glorify the name of your God" (2 Nephi 6:4).

Dr. Parry's career, defined by his world-renowned work with the Dead Sea Scrolls and his decades of teaching at Brigham Young University, uniquely positions him to peel back the linguistic layers of the text. As a member of the International Team of Translators of the Dead Sea Scrolls, he was granted direct access to the oldest surviving biblical manuscripts in the world. This expertise is on full display here, particularly his work with the Great Isaiah Scroll (1QIsa). Drawing upon these ancient readings, Dr. Parry clarifies passages that have long been obscured in later versions—such as restoring the "seer" in Isaiah 21:8 and the "witnesses" in Isaiah 33:8.

For the Latter-day Saint reader, this translation offers something truly unique by viewing the Hebrew text through the lens of the Restoration. By incorporating insights from the Joseph Smith Translation and the Book of Mormon—clearly marked with brackets—he allows the reader to see how modern revelation aligns with and expands upon the ancient prophetic record.

Further, Dr. Parry utilizes his expertise in Hebrew poetics to format the text in its original parallelisms. By organizing these "rhymes of thought," he clarifies the logic of the prophet's message and helps identify the approximately sixty different speakers in the text.

This volume is more than a translation; it is a labor of love from a scholar who has spent over three decades helping others "behold [their] God." As a former student, I am honored to see his lifetime of expertise distilled into a work that—combined with his other important works on Isaiah—will undoubtedly continue to help a new generation of Saints search these things with greater clarity, purpose, and awe.

Shon D. Hopkin

Introduction

Isaiah, A Jesus Christ Focused Book

As God's prophet and seer, Isaiah wrote regarding the nature and character of God, as well as His awe-inspiring power and holiness. Isaiah also prophesied of Jesus Christ's birth, ministry, Atonement, death, and Resurrection, Second Coming, and millennial reign. Importantly, the book of Isaiah is quite singular because of its attentive focus on the LORD Jesus Christ:

- Isaiah presented the direct speech (the actual words) of the LORD [*Jehovah*] throughout Isaiah's book—the LORD speaks more than two-hundred times in Isaiah!
- Isaiah used the name LORD [*Jehovah*] 450 times in his book; additionally, there are literally hundreds of pronouns (*he*, *you*, *I*, *your*, *his*, and *my*) that refer to Him.
- Nephi wrote: "That I might more fully persuade them to believe in the Lord their Redeemer I did read unto them that which was written by the prophet Isaiah" (1 Nephi 19:23).[1]
- Several verses of Isaiah reveal that the LORD is our *Savior* and our *Redeemer*, e.g., Isaiah 43:3, 11; Isaiah 45:21; Isaiah 49:26; Isaiah 60:16, plus others.
- The book of Isaiah presents dozens of divine titles and names of the LORD, e.g., *Holy One of Israel*, *Lord God*, *Rock*, *Stone*, *Judge*, *King*, *Lawgiver*, *Prince of Peace*, *Lamb*, *Lord of Hosts*, plus others.

It is crucial to recognize that *Jehovah* (translated "LORD" in the King James Version) is "the covenant or proper name of the God of Israel" and that Jehovah Himself is none other than "the premortal Jesus Christ" (Bible Dictionary, "Jehovah"). In 2017, President Russell M. Nelson implored, "Commence tonight to consecrate a portion of your time each week to studying everything Jesus said and did as recorded in the Old Testament, for He is the Jehovah of the Old Testament."[2] In "The Living Christ: The Testimony of the Apos-

1. Citing this verse (1 Nephi 19:23), Elder Holland wrote, "We can help the whole world be 'more fully persuaded' of Christ's divinity because of our Latter-day Saint view of him as seen through the eyes of Isaiah." Jeffrey R. Holland, "'More Fully Persuaded': Isaiah's Witness of Christ's Ministry," in *Isaiah in the Book of Mormon*, ed. Donald W. Parry and John W. Welch (Provo, UT: FARMS, 1998), 2.
2. Russell M. Nelson, "Prophets, Leadership, and Divine Law," Worldwide

tles," written in 2000, the First Presidency and Quorum of the Twelve Apostles asserted that Jesus Christ was "the Great Jehovah of the Old Testament, the Messiah of the New."[3] Those who accept the teaching that Jesus Christ's premortal name was Jehovah have a completely different view regarding the prominence of Jesus Christ in Isaiah's text. As you read the name *LORD* (450 times) or the actual words of the *LORD* (200 times) in the book of Isaiah, I invite you to think of Jesus Christ in every instance!

In addition to Isaiah's important words about Jesus Christ, Isaiah wrote and prophesied on scores of significant topics, including God's judgments against wicked people and their punishments; the peace and joy that come to the righteous when they keep God's commandments; God's sacred temples and the covenants that are associated with them; the nothingness of idols and false gods and the empty outcomes of false and counterfeit worship; the Restoration of the gospel and the building of Zion in the last days; the scattering and gathering of Israel; and much more.

UNLOCKING ISAIAH'S CLOSED BOOK

Isaiah was creative and artistic when he delivered his message and prophecies to his audiences. He set forth a multitude of skillfully articulated expressions that exist in various forms, structures, and configurations—these include a great variety of poetic parallelisms and beautiful, powerful symbolic forms. While Isaiah's literary devices and techniques add vibrancy, depth, and meaning to his words, they also create certain challenges to some readers; in fact, there are three challenges that can be a deterrent for reading and understanding Isaiah's text:

1. **Poetry**. Most of the book of Isaiah is composed of poetry that is both ancient and complex. The book includes scores of poems, and a single poem may be composed of multiple two-lined parallelisms that work together to drive home a teaching or prophecy.[4] For example, Isaiah 1:2–31 forms a poem that consists of about forty-six parallelisms. In total, there are approximately 1,000 two-lined parallelisms in the book of Isaiah. Because of the background knowledge needed to understand these parallelisms, Isaiah's poetry may present a challenge to those seeking to comprehend it.

Devotional for Young Adults, January 8, 2017, Brigham Young University; see also Gordon B. Hinckley, "We Testify of Jesus Christ," *Ensign*, March 2008, 1.

3. "The Living Christ: The Testimony of the Apostles," *Ensign*, April 2000, 2.
4. For a detailed explanation regarding Isaiah's poetry and parallelisms, see Donald W. Parry, *Search Diligently the Words of Isaiah* (Provo, Utah: Religious Studies Center/Salt Lake City: Deseret Book, 2023).

2. **Different speakers.** In the book of Isaiah, there are many different speakers, or individuals whose words are expressed by Isaiah. Isaiah (as God's prophet, spokesman, and messenger) served as the speaker, narrator, and relater of history (see, for example, Isaiah 36–39); as such, Isaiah introduced many speakers in his book. While the most important and most often-cited speakers in the book of Isaiah are the Lord and the prophet Isaiah, there are about sixty different speakers in Isaiah (see below). Because of the great number of speakers, it can be difficult for us to identify the speaker in each chapter or passage.
3. **Figures of speech**. Isaiah employs scores of complex figures of speech and literary devices[5] (for example, simile, metaphor, synecdoche, metonymy, and so forth) that are often difficult for readers to comprehend. For example, the figure *simile* occurs some three hundred times in his book. Once readers understand these literary devices, they can better appreciate and understand Isaiah's text found in both the Old Testament book of Isaiah, which consists of sixty-six chapters (or 1,292 verses), and the multiple chapters and verses in the Book of Mormon in which Isaiah is quoted or paraphrased.

How important is a knowledge of figures of speech?

Bullinger explains, "It is most important to notice these. It is absolutely necessary for true interpretation. . . . Ignorance of Figures of speech has led to the grossest errors, which have been caused either from taking literally what is figurative, or from taking figurative what is literal."[6]

The three challenges listed above seem to make the book of Isaiah a closed one—as though readers need a special key to understand its contents. However, unlocking this closed book requires practices such as serious study, devoted time, prayer, and attention to the Holy Ghost, who reveals truths to us.

Dead Sea Scrolls and Medieval Hebrew Manuscripts

This new translation is based on ancient Hebrew scrolls and texts, especially the Dead Sea Scrolls (hereafter abbreviated DSS) and the Masoretic Text (Codex Leningrad B 19[A] and other medieval manuscripts).[7] The DSS, discov-

---

5. For a detailed list of 44 figures of speech together with explanations in the book of Isaiah, see Donald W. Parry, "Unlocking Isaiah's Closed Book: Figures of Speech, Literary Devices, and Writing Techniques," In *Steadfast in Defense of Faith: Essays in Honor of Daniel Peterson* (Orem, UT: Interpreter Foundation, 2023), 331–383.
6. E. W. Bullinger, *Appendixes to the Companion Bible* (Windber, PA: Bible Student's Press, 2017), 5.
7. For the intricacies that are connected to the Dead Sea Scrolls copies of Isaiah and

ered between the years 1947 and 1956, are significant finds, signaling one of the most remarkable archaeological discoveries of the twentieth century. The scrolls predate by approximately 1,000 years the medieval copies of the Masoretic Text, which was used by the translators of the King James Version and other translations of the Old Testament.

The Qumran Caves, located near the northwestern area of the Dead Sea (hence the name "Dead Sea Scrolls"), yielded 21 copies of the book of Isaiah—two from Cave 1, 18 from Cave 4, and one from Cave 5. These 21 copies date from between the years 175 BC and 74 AD. An additional copy of Isaiah (making a total of 22 copies) was discovered south of Qumran in a cave at Wadi Murabba'at. All 22 copies of Isaiah are written in Hebrew.[8] Unfortunately, most of these scrolls are severely damaged and fragmented, owing to long-term exposure to the elements.

The Isaiah scrolls present a view of what biblical manuscripts looked like at the end of the Second Temple era. Unlike the Masoretic Text, with its system of vowels, accents, punctuation, verses, and chapters, the Isaiah scrolls feature handwritten manuscripts without these helpful items (punctuation, vowels, etc.). Additionally, the scrolls sometimes contain interlinear or marginal corrections, scribal marks and notations, a different paragraphing system, and special morphological and orthographic (spelling) features.

The Isaiah scrolls have greatly impacted our understanding of the textual history of the Bible, and in recent decades, Bible translation committees have incorporated a number of these readings into their translations.[9] Here are three examples:

> *Isaiah 14:4*: "How has the oppressor ceased." One of the DSS has "oppressor" rather than the unexpected "golden city."
>
> *Isaiah 21:8*: "And the seer cried, 'My lord, I stand continually upon the watchtower all day, and I am stationed at my post all night.'" Note that one of the DSS attests "seer" rather than the unexpected "lion."

---

the Masoretic Text of Isaiah, see Donald W. Parry, *Exploring the Isaiah Scrolls and Their Textual Variants* (Leiden: Brill, 2020), including the bibliography. For the Hebrew transcriptions of the Great Isaiah Scroll, see Donald W. Parry and Elisha Qimron, *The Great Isaiah Scroll 1QIsa^{a}: A New Edition* (Leiden: Brill, 1998), including the bibliography.

8. Scholars have labeled these scrolls as follows: 1QIsa^{a} (or the Great Isaiah Scroll), 1QIsa^{b} (1Q8), 4QIsa^{a} (4Q55), 4QIsa^{b} (4Q56), 4QIsa^{c} (4Q57), 4QIsa^{d} (4Q58), 4QIsa^{e} (4Q59), 4QIsa^{f} (4Q60), 4QIsa^{g} (4Q61), 4QIsa^{h} (4Q62), 4QIsa^{i} (4Q62a), 4QIsa^{j} (4Q63), 4QIsa^{k} (4Q64), 4QIsa^{l} (4Q65), 4QIsa^{m} (4Q66), 4QIsa^{n} (4Q67), 4QIsa^{o} (4Q68), 4QpapIsa^{p} (4Q69), 4QIsa^{q} (4Q69a), 4QIsa^{r} (4Q69b), and 5QIsa (5Q3).
9. For an investigation of the utilization of biblical Qumran texts in modern translations, consult Scanlin, *Dead Sea Scrolls and Modern Translations of the Old Testament.*

Isaiah 33:8: "covenants are broken, witnesses are despised." Note that one of the DSS attests "witnesses" rather than the unexpected "cities."

THE HEBREW BIBLE AND THE HEBREW BIBLE LEXICONS

For the new translation of Isaiah, I scrutinized the following scholarly editions of the Hebrew Bible and the Dead Sea Scrolls (arranged by date of publication):

1. Elliger, Karl and Wilhelm Rudolph, eds. *Biblia Hebraica Stuttgartensia* (Stuttgart: Deutsche Bibelgesellschaft, 1983); features the Hebrew text and a critical apparatus that contains variant readings from other Hebrew manuscripts and ancient texts of Isaiah.
2. Goshen-Gottstein, Moshe H. *The Hebrew University Bible. The Book of Isaiah* (Jerusalem: Hebrew University and Magnes, 1995); features the Hebrew text and multiple critical apparatuses.
3. Parry, Donald W. and Elisha Qimron, *The Great Isaiah Scroll (1QIsa[a]): A New Edition* (STDJ 32. Leiden: Brill, 1999); sets forth a new edition of the Great Isaiah Scroll with facsimiles of the Great Isaiah Scroll and Hebrew transcriptions.
4. Ulrich, Eugene C., Martin G. Abegg, Jr., and Peter W. Flint, eds. *Qumran Cave 1.II: The Isaiah Scrolls. Part 1: Plates and Transcriptions; Part 2: Introductions, Commentary, and Textual Variants* (DJD 32. Oxford: Clarendon, 2010); sets forth plates, transcriptions, and Hebrew textual variants.
5. Parry, Donald W. *Exploring the Isaiah Scrolls and Their Textual Variants* (Leiden: E. J. Brill, 2020); presents Hebrew textual variants of the DSS versus the Masoretic Text together with possible explanations as to why the variants exist.

Also, for the new translation of Isaiah, I consulted the following four Hebrew Bible lexicons/dictionaries (all top-tier lexicons in biblical studies):

1. Brown, Francis, Samuel R. Driver, and Charles A. Briggs, *A Hebrew and English Lexicon of the Old Testament* (Oxford: Clarendon, 1977).
2. Botterweck, G. Johannes, et al. *Theological Dictionary of the Old Testament*. 17 volumes (Grand Rapids, Mich.: Eerdmans, 1974–2021).
3. Koehler, Ludwig and Walter Baumgartner, *The Hebrew and Aramaic Lexicon of the Old Testament*, 4 vols. (Leiden: Brill, 1994–1999).
4. Clines, David J. A. ed. *The Dictionary of Classical Hebrew*, 9 vols. (Sheffield, England: Sheffield Academic Press, 1993–2012).

Readings from the Joseph Smith Translation and the Book of Mormon

There are dozens of variant readings in the Book of Mormon and the Joseph Smith Translation (JST) of Isaiah.[10] Major readings (and many minor readings) are incorporated into this volume. I have utilized brackets [ ] to indicate readings from the JST and Book of Mormon. Some words have been modernized, such as *thou*, *ye*, *saith*, and so forth. Sometimes the JST reading is aligned with the Hebrew translation, so my new translation reflects both the Hebrew and the JST, but no brackets are used, for example, "How long, O Lord? And he said" (Isaiah 6:11). "Said" is found in the JST, and the equivalent word is in the Hebrew Bible, so I present it without the brackets (versus KJV's "and he answered").

Why Study Isaiah?

There may be dozens of reasons why one should embark on a serious study of Isaiah's writings—to feel the Spirit, to come to know God and His divine ways, to gain knowledge regarding ancient Israelite people and their history and culture, to better understand doctrine, for spiritual purposes, and so forth. Some individuals may read Isaiah while seeking answers to life's questions or guidance through life's challenges, knowing that sacred scripture can provide answers; scripture also provides readers with hope and faith.

In point of fact, there are six ways to read Isaiah, or six outlooks. These are:

1. Reading Isaiah in his historical context (also called a "near view"), contemporaneous with Isaiah's time
2. Reading prophecy, or a distant (into the future) view
3. Dual or multiple fulfilment prophecies (reading a near view and a distant view)
4. Likening Isaiah's words to us and others
5. Reading a passage of scripture for personal reasons (for instruction, spiritual guidance, devotionalistic purposes, to receive personal revelation, or for other reasons)
6. Reading Isaiah to understand doctrine

Beyond these six outlooks, the Book of Mormon includes several specific reasons why each of us should study Isaiah. The following list details 10 rea-

---

10. Regarding the JST, see Kent P. Jackson, Robert J. Matthews, and Scott H. Faulring. *Joseph Smith's New Translation of the Bible; Original Manuscripts* (Provo, Utah: Religious Studies Center, Brigham Young University, 2004). This work sets forth the coming forth and history of the Joseph Smith Translation (JST) as well as other matters of import that pertain to the JST—its doctrinal contributions, the scribes who were involved, their transcription methods, the time sequence to bring it forth, and more.

sons; in my view, the first three are of prime import, because they pertain to Jesus Christ.

1. Jesus Christ commanded us to study Isaiah's words: "Behold, they [the words of Isaiah] are written, ye have them before you, therefore search them" (3 Nephi 20:11) and "behold, I say unto you, that ye ought to search these things. Yea, a commandment I give unto you that ye search these things diligently; for great are the words of Isaiah" (3 Nephi 23:1; see also Mormon 8:23).
2. Isaiah's writings persuade us to "learn and glorify the name of our God" (2 Nephi 6:4).
3. Isaiah was a special witness of Jesus Christ—he saw the Redeemer (2 Nephi 11:2; see also Isaiah 6:1).
4. Isaiah spoke concerning the scattering and gathering of the house of Israel (1 Nephi 15:20). Jesus explained, "For surely [Isaiah] spake as touching all things concerning my people which are of the house of Israel; therefore, it must needs be that he must speak also to the Gentiles" (3 Nephi 23:2).
5. Isaiah's prophecies will be fulfilled. Jesus testified, "All things that [Isaiah] spake have been and shall be, even according to the words which he spake" (3 Nephi 23:3).
6. Nephi taught that Isaiah's words are for "our profit and learning" (1 Nephi 19:23). Manifestly, those who regularly and sincerely search the book of Isaiah will profit and learn more.
7. Isaiah taught many aspects of God's judgments (divine punishments), or His prophetic warnings to cities and nations (see 2 Nephi 25:6). In fact, several chapters of Isaiah consist of God's judgments (i.e., chapters 13–17, 23). By studying these matters, we can learn much regarding the way God deals with wicked communities and nations.
8. Isaiah's writings encourage us to be joyful "for all men"; Nephi wrote, "And now I write some of the words of Isaiah, that whoso of my people shall see these words may lift up their hearts and rejoice for all men" (2 Nephi 11:8).
9. Isaiah's writings are of "great worth unto them in the last days" (2 Nephi 25:8). Why? Because many of his prophecies will be fulfilled in our day and we will be witnesses of their fulfillment.
10. Isaiah's writings may be likened unto us, who are members of the house of Israel. Nephi explained, "Wherefore, they [Isaiah's words] may be likened unto you, for ye are of the house of Israel. And there are many things which have been spoken by Isaiah which may be likened unto you, because ye are of the house of

Israel" (2 Nephi 6:5; 2 Nephi 11:2, 8). It is a productive, profitable, and sacred exercise for us to liken Isaiah's words to us.

The Man Named Isaiah

Isaiah was a prophet and seer who ministered between the years circa 740 and 700 BC (or perhaps 699 BC or even later—scholars do not always agree on the dates of Isaiah's ministry). His father's name was Amoz (1:1), not to be confused with the prophet Amos. Isaiah lived and prophesied in Jerusalem, during the reigns of Kings Uzziah, Jotham, Ahaz, and Hezekiah (1:1). Isaiah personally knew some or all these kings (see Isaiah 7:3; 38:1–8). Several Old Testament chapters provide us with information regarding Isaiah and his ministry (Isaiah 36–39, 2 Kings 14–20, and 2 Chronicles 26–32). Isaiah was married to the "prophetess" (8:3; we do not know her name), and they were the parents of at least two children—Shear-jashub and Maher-shalal-hash-baz.

Isaiah was a prophet to many nations and kingdoms and he specifically prophesied concerning Judah (Isaiah 3:1–12), the Northern Kingdom of Israel (9:8–10:4), Assyria (10:12–19), Babylon (13:6–22; 21:1–10; 47:1–15), the Philistines (14:28–32), Moab (15:1–16:4), Egypt (19:1–25), Arabia (21:13–17), Edom (34:1–15), and others. Isaiah's words, of course, are relevant throughout the ages to all nations and peoples.

Isaiah's Book

Isaiah wrote his book in Hebrew (what we now call *Biblical Hebrew*), which lacked upper case letters, punctuation, or chapters and verses (these were later inventions, although Isaiah's original writings and revelations may have had some form of a paragraph system). Isaiah's book, as we have it at the present time, is divided into 1292 verses and 66 chapters. This system of chapters and verses assists us as we study, teach, and cross-reference Isaiah's words with other scriptural texts. Many people throughout the centuries have considered Hebrew to be a sacred language because God used it to reveal His word to prophets, seers, and others during the Old Testament period. The oldest extant Hebrew texts of Isaiah are those belonging to the Dead Sea Scrolls, which date between the years 175 BC and 74 AD. However, the Isaiah texts in the Book of Mormon belong to an earlier period than the Dead Sea Scrolls; God revealed the Book of Mormon Isaiah texts to the Prophet Joseph Smith, as he translated them from the golden plates through the gift and power of God.

The Art of Translating

After concluding my academic training, which included extensive study at the Hebrew University of Jerusalem, Israel, I have been blessed to teach full-time at Brigham Young University for more than three decades. My teaching responsibilities include instructing students to read and translate Biblical Hebrew (the Hebrew of the Old Testament), Qumran Hebrew (the Hebrew of the Dead Sea Scrolls), and Mishnaic Hebrew (the Hebrew of the Mishnah). My first and primary responsibility is teaching Biblical Hebrew. In addition to teaching, I conduct research on the Hebrew Bible and the Dead Sea Scrolls and publish my findings in scholarly articles and books. These scholarly works are distributed in various venues to a worldwide audience, including in academic and research libraries. I also present my findings at academic conferences, congresses, and symposia in many parts of the world.

In January 1994, I was invited to serve as a member of the International Team of Translators of the Dead Sea Scrolls. This opportunity and privilege gave me direct access to the actual scrolls, housed first in the Rockefeller Archeological Museum (27 Sultan Suleiman Street, Jerusalem, Israel) and years later in the Israel Museum (Ruppin Blvd. 11, Jerusalem, Israel). Although I have researched and studied many of the Dead Sea Scrolls—both biblical and nonbiblical—my primary focus as an academic over the decades has been the books of Isaiah and 1 and 2 Samuel (my bibliography of published academic articles and books is widely available). Later I served on the Board of Directors of the Dead Sea Scrolls Foundation (2014–2025). In this capacity I continued to form lasting relationships with Dead Sea Scrolls' scholars from the international community of translators.

Moreover, over the decades I have read and translated Isaiah from the Hebrew Bible with my students at Brigham Young University. During the semester, we discuss the meaning of this ancient Hebrew word or that Hebrew phrase, in its context, with the objective of learning its meaning as Isaiah intended it. Sometimes we determine that there are two or three ways to legitimately render Hebrew words into English; so, I explain to my students: "It is not because Hebrew is such a fluid language, rather, the challenge is rendering the Hebrew into idiomatic English." I continue to explain to my students, "That is to say, once you are well equipped to deal with Biblical Hebrew, the challenge of translation pertains to the target language (in this case, the English language), not the original Hebrew. Isaiah makes perfect sense (most of the time) in Hebrew, which was Isaiah's original language. But how can we make it readable in English?" So, with these things in mind, I want to remind readers that there are different, legitimate ways to translate Isaiah's Hebrew into twenty-first-century English. And nowhere do I claim that my translation is the end-all, definitive rendering of Isaiah's words.

Similarly, my interpretation of some of Isaiah's symbols or words is informed by my knowledge and understanding of the Gospel of Jesus Christ, as a member of The Church of Jesus Christ of Latter-day Saints. I view Isaiah and interpret his writings through the lens of the Gospel of Jesus Christ, the Restoration, and modern Prophets and Apostles. Scholars of other faiths and religious traditions, of course, sometimes assign different interpretations to Isaiah's symbols or words. That is the very nature of scholarship, translational approaches, and biblical interpretation.

MY METHODOLOGY FOR THE NEW TRANSLATION

This volume has been prepared, presented, and formatted to help readers better understand Isaiah. While doing so, I have also followed certain practices:

1) Providing Titles for Smaller Literary Units

To make this volume more manageable and Isaiah's words easier to comprehend, I have divided Isaiah's sixty-six chapters into scores of smaller literary units (which scholars call *pericopes*). I have provided titles for each of these smaller literary units. For example, I have labeled Isaiah 2:6–9 as "Isaiah's Address (Prayer) to the LORD'; Isaiah 3:1–12 as "Woe to the Wicked! Hope for the Righteous!"; and Isaiah 5:1–7 as "The Song of the Vineyard." These titles are suggestions only; as individuals study Isaiah, they may come up with titles that they feel are more appropriate.

Generally, these smaller units are thematically linked with the preceding units as well as the units that follow. Therefore, each literary unit should be read in its greater context, in other words, with both the previous and the following units.

2) Formatted Two-Lined Parallelisms

To assist the reader in locating, identifying, and comprehending Isaiah's difficult poetry, I have formatted most of his writings into two-lined parallelisms and, where applicable, three- or four-line parallelisms. Each parallelism is followed by a space. Although I attempted to present all of Isaiah's parallelisms, undoubtedly, I did not locate all of them because some of them are quite subtle. Furthermore, because of the restrictions of the 6" x 9" formatting of the book, there are dozens of occasions that I was unable to properly format parallelisms into two lines. Note that my formatting of the parallelisms are suggestions only. As individuals diligently search Isaiah's writings, they may determine different parallelistic structures and formations.

Most of Isaiah's book is composed of ancient poetry, which consists of parallelisms and other blocks of scripture. Like numerous examples of modern poetry, Isaiah's poetry displays qualities of beauty as well as a power to influence our emotions and sensibilities. But Isaiah's poetry has a different character than modern poetry, which sometimes features rhyming schemes and other distinctive approaches.

So, what is a parallelism? A parallelism generally consists of two lines, although three- and four-lined cases do exist. Most parallelisms, therefore, are very short. Line 1 sets forth an important truth, and then line 2 broadens, restates, or punctuates the truth of line 1. We would state that the two lines are parallel with each other (hence, the term poetic "parallelism"); they correspond with each other in some way; and they are thematically tied together in a unified manner. The following examples of parallelisms will serve to introduce this poetic phenomenon to the reader. The first three of the following examples are called synonymous parallelisms, because expressions in the two lines feature synonyms (or, near synonyms):

> "Israel did not know,
> My people did not understand." (1:3)

In this two-lined parallelism, "Israel" parallels "My people," and "did not know" is analogous to "did not understand."

> "Every head is sick;
> Every heart is diseased." (1:5)

In this two-lined parallelism, "Every head" corresponds with "Every heart" (*head* and *heart* are both body parts) and "sick" parallels "diseased."

> "Your land is desolate,
> Your cities are burned with fire." (1:7)

This two-line parallelism features corresponding geographical terms ("land" and "cities") as well as words that describe destruction ("desolate" and "burned with fire").

Isaiah also wrote parallelisms that feature opposites (called antithetical parallelisms). For instance,

> "If you are willing and obedient, you will eat the good things of the land;
> but if you refuse and rebel, by the sword you will be eaten." (1:19–20)

In this example, Isaiah contrasts terms or ideas in the two lines: "willing and obedient" in line 1 stands opposite to "refuse and rebel" in line 2; also, "you will eat the good things of the land" contrasts with "by the sword you will be eaten."

Another example of a parallelism that features opposites:

> "Behold, My servants will sing with gladness of heart,
> but you will cry out for pain of heart" (65:14).

In this passage, "sing" stands opposite of "cry out" and "gladness of heart" is contrary to "pain of heart."

Elsewhere I have examined in detail a host of different categories or configurations of parallelisms that exist in Isaiah. These include the following configurations: synonymous parallelisms, antithetical parallelisms, emblematic parallelisms, parallelisms with identical words or phrases, gender-matched parallelisms, rhetorical questions parallelisms, parallelisms showing progression, numbers parallelisms, resultative relationship parallelisms, parallelisms with lists, and phonological parallelisms.

Additionally, Isaiah produced a host of linguistic and grammatical parallelisms. These include parallelisms featuring masculine and feminine nouns, parallelisms with specific word order, parallelisms that feature identical

Hebrew verbal roots, parallelisms that feature different inflections of an identical Hebrew verbal root, parallelisms that feature a singular demonstrative adjective versus a plural demonstrative adjective, parallelisms that feature a singular verb versus plural verb, parallelisms that feature antithetical adjectives, parallelisms that feature a positive versus a negative statement, parallelisms that feature feminine and masculine adjectives of the same root, and parallelisms that feature a contrast in grammatical mood.[11]

An in-depth study of Isaiah's parallelisms would take a lifetime. This is because Isaiah masterfully and artistically wrote poetry that may well be without equal in history. As we study Isaiah's poetry, we can learn more about how he presented his parallelisms in a variety of configurations. But the mechanics of parallelisms is just the beginning; the next step is to study Isaiah's parallelisms in order to bring to light his crucial doctrinal messages regarding Jesus Christ and His atonement, the restoration of the Gospel, God's judgments against the wicked, the building of Zion, the prophecies concerning the Last Days and the Millennium, and much, much more. We must always move beyond the mechanics to seek out and learn of Isaiah's doctrinal messages and how Isaiah's words apply to each of us. And we cannot forget to pray and to inquire of the Lord, "what does Isaiah mean here, in this passage, to Isaiah's ancient community?" And "what do Isaiah's words mean to me, in the twenty-first century?"

3) Pronouns that Refer to God

I have capitalized all pronouns that refer to God (*Me*, *My*, *You*, *Your*, *He*, *Him*) in order to (a) reverence Him with the highest regard, by separating Him from all other characters in the text, and (b) to help the reader know when God is the speaker, thus making the text easier to comprehend.

4) Multiple "Speakers" in the Book of Isaiah[12]

In the book of Isaiah, there are many different speakers, or individuals who express words. Time after time, Isaiah (as God's prophet, spokesman, and messenger) served as the speaker, narrator, and relater of history (see, for example, Isaiah 36–39); Isaiah also had the important role of introducing other speakers. In this book I offer suggestions (throughout this new translation in the left-hand column, in bold letters) regarding who the speakers are, but many of my suggestions are tentative and provisional, because we are not

---

11. All of these categories of parallelisms are presented and discussed in *Search Diligently the Words of Isaiah.*
12. This entire book is copyright protected by National and International copyright conventions and treaties; this includes my methodology for determining different speakers and my identification of speakers in the book of Isaiah. For more information, consult the U.S. Copyright office.

always certain who the speaker is. In the end, each student of Isaiah will have to determine this matter for themselves.

I will now set forth, in very abbreviated format, some of the points of my methodology:

a) On several occasions, Isaiah and others address the Lord directly in a speech form called the vocative, e.g., "O LORD." In most of these cases, it is somewhat clear who the speaker is. For example, Isaiah 37:15–16 states, "And Hezekiah prayed to the LORD, saying, O LORD of Hosts, the God of Israel, enthroned on the cherubim..." In this case, the speaker is clearly Hezekiah, so we attribute verses 16-20 to Hezekiah (see **Hezekiah** in bold in the left margin).
b) Sometimes the Lord introduces Himself with the words "I am the Lord" (42:8; 43:3, 11, 15; 44:24; 45:3, 5–6; 45:18; 49:22; 51:15; 60:16, 22) and "I, the LORD" (27:3; 41:13, 17; 42:6; 45:8, 19, 21; 61:8). These self-identification statements make it evident that He is the speaker.
c) The book of Isaiah regularly attests prophetic speech forms that introduce the Lord as the speaker. These speech forms include the follow expressions: "thus saith the Lord," "the LORD has spoken," "Hear the word of the LORD," "says the LORD," "the Lord declares," and others. For instance, in Isaiah 10:24, the prophet introduces the Lord's words by writing, "Therefore thus *says* the Lord" (italics added; see also 7:7; 18:4; 22:15; 30:12, and so forth). He also uses other speech forms. These speech formulas also indicate Isaiah's prophetic authority to speak in the name of the Lord. It should be noted that it is often difficult to know if the Lord or Isaiah is using these speech forms, so our identification remains tentative.
d) Both the Lord and Isaiah use various expressions when they introduce other speakers, such as "saying," "say," "said," "declares," "called," "spoke," "this song will be sung," and similar terms. For example, Isaiah 4:1 states, "And in that day, seven women will grasp one man, saying ..." In this case, it is clear that the speakers are seven women, so we place **Seven Women** in bold in the left-hand margin.
e) Sometimes the identification of the speaker is unclear, but clues in the text help us to make an identification. These clues include the greater context of the speaker's words, the content and meaning of the passage, and much more.
f) Isaiah sometimes uses divine titles when he refers to the Lord, such as LORD, *LORD of Hosts*, *God*, LORD *God of Israel*, *Maker*, *Holy One of Israel*, and many others. Isaiah also refers to the Lord using third person pronouns, "He" and "Him." In such cases, I

> identify "**Isaiah**" as the speaker. For example, I identify Isaiah as the speaker in the following three cases: "the Lord, the Lord of Hosts, removes from Jerusalem and from Judah" (3:1); "The Lord takes His place to plead a cause" (3:13); and "Wail, for the day of the Lord is near; it will come as destruction from the Almighty" (13:6). The Lord Himself may be the speaker in these passages, and as well, He may be the speaker throughout the book of Isaiah, because He is the source of revelation to His prophet and seer, Isaiah.

There are a large variety and assortment of speakers in Isaiah. These include righteous persons, such as "God's covenant people," "Christ's disciples," "worshippers," and "the righteous"; as well as evil characters, including "the wicked," "idolaters," "haters," "men of scorning," "wicked leaders," and "Lucifer." Isaiah writings also present the words of individuals who would be born in later dispensations. Although Isaiah does not name them, a careful reading of the text suggests that these include John the Baptist, Joseph Smith, Martin Harris, and Charles Anthon (these speakers are often based on our comprehension of the scriptures [see for example, JST Isaiah 29] and statements of Latter-day Saint Prophets and Apostles). Isaiah also presents several unusual and perhaps unexpected speakers, such as clay (see 45:9), "dead spirits," "Babylon," "Thing formed," "Lady Zion," and others. For example, in Isaiah 49:14, Lady Zion speaks these words,

Lady Zion "The LORD has forsaken me,
and my Lord has forgotten me."

The top two speakers, in terms of both importance and quantity, are the Lord (about 216 times) and the prophet Isaiah (about 344 times). Altogether, there are about sixty different speakers in Isaiah (but if we count the twenty-three "Unnamed individual[s]" as separate persons, then the number is approximately eighty-three). Isaiah presents the approximately sixty speakers about seven-hundred times. For the list, see the table below. This great number helps us to comprehend how exacting Isaiah's writings are and how the prophet was so methodical in his presentation. In fact, the identification of the various speakers tends to make Isaiah's writings easier to understand. When we, the readers of Isaiah, identify these various speakers and read their words in the context of other speakers, we can more skillfully comprehend Isaiah's writings.

The different speakers in Isaiah are listed—highest number first, then in descending order. Although I have attempted to identify most of the speakers in Isaiah, we should all remember that *all* of Isaiah's text is written to and for every generation of readers! Every student and reader of Isaiah—from Isaiah's day until our own time—can benefit from his words; that is to say, from the first verse of Isaiah (1:1) to the very last (66:24), each of us can benefit from the Lord's word as He revealed it to His prophet and seer, Isaiah.

Isaiah	344	Seraph	2	Military leader	1
The LORD	216	Thing formed	2	One who properly fasts	1
Unnamed individual(s)	23	Ahaz	1	People of stature	1
God's covenant people	21	Bereaved children	1	Reveler	1
The wicked	10	Clay (substance)	1	Samaria's people	1
Hezekiah	9	Dead spirits	1	Seven women	1
Idolater(s)	7	Eliakim and Shebna	1	Singers	1
Babylon	4	Eliakim, Shebna, and Joah	1	The righteous	1
Chief officer	4	Eunuch	1	Titles of Lady Zion	1
Christ's disciples	4	Foreigner	1	Titles of Lord's people	1
Non-believers	4	Former oppressors	1	Tormenters	1
Inhabitants of Judah	3	Haters	1	Trees	1
Worshipper(s)	3	Herald	1	Tyre	1
Zion's inhabitants	3	Holy Ghost	1	Unnamed mourner	1
Assyria's king	2	Individual from Seir	1	Watchman	1
C. Anthon	2	J. Smith	1	Wicked leaders	1
Lady Zion	2	John the Baptist	1	Witnesses	1
M. Harris	2	Kings	1	Written on unnamed individual's hand	1
Messiah	2	Lucifer	1		
People	2	Men of scorning	1		

5) Translating Hebrew words into English

The Hebrew lexicons demonstrate that there are occasions when one Hebrew word may be rendered into different English words; for example, the Hebrew conjunction *waw* may be translated as "and" or "but." So, too, in this translation, I have sometimes rendered certain Hebrew words into different English words, according to the context of the passage.

Many Hebrew words in Isaiah are difficult to translate because we remain uncertain as to their exact meaning. A few wild animals and some types of trees and plants especially fall into this category.

6) Retaining Hebraisms in My Translation

In my translation of Isaiah, I have attempted to retain many of the Hebraisms and Hebrew-like expressions, including the following: "and it came to pass," the many "ands," the construct form "House of the Lord" instead of "Lord's House" (there are hundreds of these construct forms), idea-amplifying plurals, ancient idiomatic expressions (even when they are rather difficult to comprehend), and so forth.

7) Avoidance of Archaic Forms

Except for a couple of blocks of text from the JST in Isaiah 29, I have avoided using various archaic forms, such as *thee*, *thou*, *ye*, *saith*, and so forth. These archaic forms are sometimes difficult for younger or inexperienced readers to comprehend. The Hebrew Bible does not have two sets of pronouns like we do in English: *you* and *thou*, *your* and *thy*, and so forth.

8) Scriptural References

Unless otherwise noted, all scriptural references in parentheses are from Isaiah; for example (53:1) means (Isaiah 53:1).

9) Translating the Divine Name Yahweh

The Hebrew *Yahweh*, from which we have the name *Jehovah*, is translated "LORD" (in all uppercase letters). The convention to employ *LORD* rather than *Jehovah* was held by many early English translations of the Old Testament, including the King James Version. Contrast LORD with "Lord" (lowercase letters), which originates from the Hebrew *adonai*. The convention to employ *Lord* was also held by many early English translations of the Old Testament, including the King James Version. Both LORD (*Yahweh*) and Lord (*adonai*) are found throughout Isaiah's writings.

10) The Usage of quotation marks

This translation employs quotation marks at certain places, especially when introduced with such terms as "saying," "say," "said," "declares," and others. The intent of quotation marks is to help to clarify who the speakers are. Just as the identification of the speaker(s) sometimes remain provisional, the usage of quotation marks also remains tentative.

Three Related Works on Isaiah

My new translation—*A New Translation of Isaiah Based on Ancient Scrolls and Texts*—completes a group of three related works on Isaiah. Previously, I published the following introduction of Isaiah: *Search Diligently the Words of Isaiah* (Provo, Utah: Religious Studies Center/Salt Lake City: Deseret Book, 2023); and before that, three of us—Donald W. Parry, Jay A. Parry, and Tina Peterson—wrote a verse-by-verse commentary of the entire book of Isaiah, *Understanding Isaiah* (Salt Lake City: Deseret Book, 1998). It is hoped that the three related works on Isaiah will encourage each of us to search Isaiah's writings to "learn and glorify the name of our God" (2 Nephi 6:4).

Archaic Language in Early English Bible Translations

Early English translations of the Bible, such as those by Wycliffe (ca. 1384), Tyndale (1530), Coverdale (1535), Matthew (1537), and Bishop (1568), as well as the King James Version (1611), contain archaic (old-fashioned and obsolete) words. While such words were generally accurate translations from the original language, they are now out of date, and they frequently obscure the meaning of the text. Archaisms from the King James Version of the book of Isaiah appear in verb forms (e.g., *art, wilt, shalt, hath, doth, hast, wast, astonied, beget, beseech, bestead, bewail, bewray, clave, contemned, extolled, overpast, plaister, reckoned, shew, trodden, wrought*), in *-st* suffixed verbs (e.g., *didst, sayest, dwellest, shouldest, camest, bringest, abhorrest, comfortedst*), in *-th* suffixed verbs (e.g., *stirreth, heweth, graveth, scattereth, mourneth, fadeth, languisheth, endeth, fleeth, cometh, swimmeth, spreadeth, keepeth, layeth, crieth, heweth, kindleth, saith, standeth, hindereth, abhorreth*), in transliterations of Hebrew terms (e.g., *homer, ephah, cherubims*), in personal pronouns (e.g., *thou, thee, thy, ye, thine, thyself*), in nouns (e.g., *besom, bullocks, cauls, divorcement, enchantments, eveningtide, exactors, feller, firebrands, flagons, gin, hireling, lees, mirth, mufflers, rereward, silverlings, soothsayers, stomacher, tabret, tow, traffickers, wimples*), in exclamations (e.g., *ho, lo*), prepositions (e.g., *betwixt*), in adjectives (e.g., *doleful, hoar, stouthearted, sucking* [child], *wroth*), and in adverbs (e.g., *frowardly, hither, thence, thither, whence, whereto, wherewith*).

Archaic expressions from Isaiah include (followed by a modern translation in parentheses): "hardly bestead and hungry" ("distressed and hungry," 8:21), "dimness of anguish" ("gloom of anguish," 8:22), "bewray not him that wandereth" ("do not betray the fugitives," 16:3), "for the extortioner is at an end, the spoiler ceaseth" ("when the oppressor exists no more, destruction ceases," 16:4), "they prevented with their bread him that fled" ("bring bread to the fugitives," 21:14), "bunches of camels" ("humps of camels," 30:5), and "ear the ground" ("plow the ground," 30:24). Such examples could be multiplied.

Many archaic expressions are puzzling because their current meanings are different from what they were 400 years ago. For example, *carriage* (10:28) referred to "something that is carried," such as gear or supplies, but now *carriage* refers to "a wheeled vehicle"; *corn* (17:5; 21:10) used to mean "grain" but now corn refers to "maize"; *cunning* (3:3; 40:20) meant "skillful" but cunning now means "sly"; *durable clothing* (23:18) referred to "splendid clothing" but now means "clothing that lasts a long time"; *meat* (62:8) was a generic term for "food" but now it refers to "the flesh of animals"; a *mean man* (2:9) meant a "common man" but now it denotes of "a cruel man." Other archaisms that have changed meaning include the words *prevent* (21:14), *let* (43:13), and *debate* (58:4).

The present translation attempts to avoid archaic and obsolete expressions; and the personal pronouns *thou, thee, thy, ye, thine,* and *thyself* that appear in the phrases of the Joseph Smith Translation and Book of Mormon cited in the translation have generally been updated.

This New Translation Does Not Replace the King James Version

In my profession, I have taught the King James Version of the Bible (KJV) for decades; it is a favorite and best-loved translation, in part because it is a majestic, beautiful, and powerful work. For this reason, this new translation does not replace the KJV; in fact, this new translation should not be considered authoritative, official, or even semiofficial in any way. It is merely a resource for students of Isaiah, no more and no less. As a professor at Brigham Young University who was trained to read and translate the Dead Sea Scrolls, the

Hebrew Bible, and other ancient Hebrew texts, I offer this translation as my work alone. I do not represent The Church of Jesus Christ of Latter-day Saints or Brigham Young University. Any mistranslation, misrepresentation, or typographical error is my responsibility.

Abbreviations and Symbols

DSS Isaiah	Refers to one or more of the Dead Sea Scrolls books of Isaiah
JST	Joseph Smith Translation
KJV	King James Version
MT	Masoretic Text of the Bible (the Hebrew Bible)
[ ]	Indicates a reading from JST Isaiah or Book of Mormon Isaiah
{ }	Indicates explanatory words that are not found in the Hebrew texts but are added to the translation to make sense of the verse, as in 14:25.

Isaiah: A New Translation

The Vision of Isaiah–Introduction (1:1)

Isaiah

1 1 The vision of Isaiah, the son of Amoz, which he saw concerning Judah and Jerusalem during the days of Uzziah, Jotham, Ahaz, and Hezekiah—kings of Judah.

God Charges Israel for Its Sins (1:2–5a)

Isaiah

2 Hear, O heavens!
And give ear, O earth! Because the Lord has spoken:

The Lord

"Children I have brought up and raised,
but they rebelled[a] against Me.

3 The ox knows its purchaser
and the ass its owner's feeding trough.

Israel did not know;
My people did not understand."

Isaiah

4 Woe! nation that sins,
people burdened with iniquity,

offspring of evildoers,
children who are corrupt.

They have abandoned[b] the Lord!
They have despised the Holy One of Israel!
They have turned their backs {on Him}!

5 Why will you be beaten again?
Why will you add rebellion?

Israel's Spiritually Sick Condition: The People (1:5b–6) and the Land (1:7–9)

Isaiah

Every head is sick;
every heart is diseased.

6 From the sole of the foot to the head, there is no healthy part.
A wound, and a slash, and a fresh blow—

they have not been closed nor wrapped,
neither softened with oil.

---

a. (Hebrew, *psh'*) also means "to transgress."
b. "abandon" (Hebrew, *'zv*) can also read "forsaken."

[7]Your land is desolate;
your cities are burned with fire.

Your soil? Strangers eat it in front of you;
it is a waste, overthrown by strangers.

[8]And the daughter of Zion is left as a hut in a vineyard,
as a temporary shelter in a cucumber field,
as a city besieged.

[9]If the Lord of Hosts[a] had not left us a few survivors,
we would have been like Sodom;
we would have been as Gomorrah.

Condemnation against Israel's Apostate Temple Practices (1:10–15)

Isaiah [10]Hear the word of the Lord, O rulers of Sodom;
give ear to the law of our God, O people of Gomorrah.

The Lord [11]"What use is the multitude of your sacrifices to Me?"

Isaiah says the Lord.

The Lord "I have eaten My fill of burnt offerings of
rams, and the fat of fatted steers,
and I do not desire the blood of bulls and lambs or male goats.

[12]When you come to see My face,
who required this from your hand to trample My courts?

[13]You will no longer bring a worthless offering;
incense, it is an abomination to Me;

new moon and Sabbath,
calling of an assembly—

I cannot endure iniquity and the sacred assembly;
[14]My soul hates your new moons and your festivals;

they have become a burden to Me;
I am weary of bearing them.

[15]And when you spread forth your palms,
I will shut My eyes from you;
even when you pray much, I will not hear.

---

a. This important title occurs sixty-two times in Isaiah. *Hosts* generally refers to God's angels—He is the Lord of a great multitude of angels. *Lord of Hosts*, here, and elsewhere, can also be translated "Lord of Armies," referring to the Lord's armies of angels.

Your hands are full of blood,
your fingers with iniquity.[a]

ISRAEL COMMANDED TO REPENT AND CLEANSE ITSELF (1:16–20)

The LORD 16 Wash!
Purify yourself!

Remove the evil of your deeds from before My eyes.
Stop the evil.

17 Learn to do good,
seek justice,

make the oppressed happy,
administer justice for the orphan,
argue the case for the widow.

18 Come, please, and let us reason together,"[b]

Isaiah says the LORD:

The LORD "If your sins are as scarlet, they will be made white like snow;
if they are red like crimson, they will be like wool.

19 If you are willing and obedient[c], you will
eat the good things of the land;
but if you refuse and rebel, by the sword you will be eaten."

Isaiah 20 For the mouth of the LORD has spoken.

LAMENT FOR THE INHABITANTS OF JERUSALEM. (1:21–24A)

Isaiah 21 How[d] the faithful town has become a
prostitute! Filled with justice;
righteousness lodged in her, but now—murderers!

22 Your silver has become dross,
your wine diluted with water.

23 Your rulers are rebels
and companions of thieves.

---

a This reading is from DSS Isaiah.

b. "reason together" is technically a legal term in the Hebrew (*ykhch*), as if the Lord is calling the people to court.

c. The Hebrew *shm'* literally means "to hear." "To hear" in Hebrew sometimes means "to obey."

d. The word *how* (Hebrew, *'ykh*) here introduces a lament, like those in the book of *Lamentations* (see Lamentations 1:1; Lamentations 2:1).

Everyone loves bribes
and chases after gifts.

24 They do not administer justice for the orphan,
neither does the case of the widow come to them.

ZION TO BE REDEEMED, THE WICKED DESTROYED (1:24B–31)

Isaiah

24 Therefore the Lord,
the LORD[a] of Hosts,
the Mighty One of Israel, declares:

The LORD

"Alas! I will get relief from My adversaries
and avenge me of My enemies.

25 And I will turn My hand upon you,
and I will smelt away your dross like lye,
and I will take away all your slag.

26 And I will restore your judges as at the first
and your counselors as at the beginning.

After this you will be called,
'The City of Righteousness,'
'The Faithful Town.'

27 Zion will be redeemed with justice
and her repentant[b] ones with righteousness.

28 But transgressors and sinners together will be crushed,
and those that forsake the LORD will perish.

29 For you will be ashamed of the oaks that you have desired,
and you will be confounded because of the
gardens that you have chosen.

30 For you will be as an oak whose leaf withers
and as a garden without water.

31 And the strong one will be as tinder
and his work as a spark,

and both will burn together,
and no one will quench them."

---

a. "Lord" in lower case letters and "LORD" in upper case letters are two different words in Hebrew. "Lord" (Hebrew, *'adon*) denotes one who have power or authority over others; *'adon* can also be translated "master." "LORD" (Hebrew, *yhwh*) is the name Jehovah in English (I am simplifying this).

b. The Hebrew *shwv* denotes both "to return" and "to repent"; therefore, when we

The Mountain (Temple) of the Lord (2:1–5)

Isaiah

2 1 The word that Isaiah, the son of Amoz, saw concerning
Judah and Jerusalem. 2 And it will come to pass in the last
days, [when][a] the mountain of the LORD's House

will be established at the top of the mountains[b],
and it will be elevated above the hills,

then all nations will flow like a river[c] to it.
3 And many peoples will come and say,

God's covenant people

"Come,
and let us go up[d]

to the mountain of the LORD,
to the House of the God of Jacob,

that He may teach[e] us of His ways
and that we may walk in His paths;

because from Zion the law will go forth,
and the word of the LORD from Jerusalem."

Isaiah

4 And He will judge among the nations,
and He will settle the case for many peoples.

And they will hammer their swords into plowshares
and their spears into pruning hooks.

And nation will not lift a sword against nation,
nor will they learn war again.

5 O house of Jacob, come, and let us walk
in the light of the LORD.
[Yea, come, for you have all gone astray,
everyone to his wicked ways.][f]

---

return to God, we are repentant.

a. Bracketed word is from JST and 2 Nephi 12:2.
b. Top (from the Hebrew *r'sh*) literally means "head"; but it also denotes the chief or highest ranking. God's temple, therefore, is a high-ranking institution—one of utmost importance and of great prominence.
c. Isaiah skillfully took the Hebrew noun for river (*nhr*) and made a verb out of it, thus the translation is literally "to river," "to flow like a river," or "to stream."
d. The Hebrew term *alah* ("go up," "ascend") is a watchword utilized by prophets in connection with individuals who ascend to God's temples.
e. The Hebrew Torah ("law") is derived from the verb "to teach."
f. Bracketed words in verse 5 are from JST, 2 Nephi 12:5.

Isaiah's Address (Prayer) to the Lord (2:6–9)

Isaiah

6 Surely, [O Lord][a], You have forsaken Your
people, the house of Jacob,
because they are filled from the east

and [hearken unto] soothsayers like the Philistines,
and they clap hands[b] with foreigners.

7 Their land is full of silver and gold,
and there is no end to their treasures.

Their land is full of horses,
and there is no end to their chariots.

8 And their land is full of idols;
they bow down to the work of their hands,
that which their fingers have made.

9 And the human has [not] bowed down,
and man has [not] been brought down; do not forgive [him].

The Day of the Lord (2:10–22)

Isaiah

10 [O you wicked ones,][c] enter the rock, and hide in the dust;
because the fear of the Lord and His majesty [will smite you].

11 [And it will come to pass that][d] the eyes of the
arrogant human will become low,
and the highness of [man][e] will bow down,

and the Lord alone will be exalted in that day.

12 For the day of the Lord of Hosts [soon
comes upon all nations][f];

[yea, upon everyone;
yea,] upon the proud and lifted,

and upon everyone who is arrogant;
but such will be brought low.

---

a. Note that the bracketed items in verses 6–9 are from the JST, 2 Nephi 12:6–9.

b. The Hebrew (*sfq*) underlying "clap hands" can also be translated "clasped hands" or "exchange handshakes," either in business or trade agreements or in false temple worship.

c. The bracketed expressions in verses 10 and 11 are from JST and 2 Nephi 12:10–11.

d. Bracketed words are from JST and 2 Nephi 12:11.

e. Bracketed word is from JST.

f. Bracketed words in verse 12 are from JST and 2 Nephi 12:12.

13 [Yea, and the day of the Lord will come][a]
upon all the cedars of Lebanon,
[for they][b] are high and elevated, and
upon all the oaks of Bashan,

14 and upon all the high mountains,
and upon all the hills

[and upon all the nations that][c] are elevated,
[and upon every people][d].

15 And upon every tall tower,
and upon every fortified wall,

16 [and upon all the ships of the sea,][e]
and upon all the ships of Tarshish,
and upon all luxury ships.

17 And the loftiness of the human will bow down,
and the height of men will be made low,

and the Lord alone will be exalted in that day.

18 And the idols will completely disappear.

19 And {people} will come into the caves of the rocks
and into the caverns of the ground,

for the fear of the Lord [will come upon them,][f]
and the glory of His majesty [will smite them]
when He arises to cause the earth to tremble.

20 In that day the human will cast away his idols of silver
and his idols of gold, which he has made for himself to worship,

to the moles
and to the bats[g],

21 to come into the crevices of the rocks
and into the clefts of the cliffs,

---

a. From JST and 2 Nephi 12:13.
b. From JST and 2 Nephi 12:13.
c. From JST and 2 Nephi 12:14.
d. From 2 Nephi 12:14.
e. From JST and 2 Nephi 12:16.
f. Bracketed words in verse 19 are from JST and 2 Nephi 12:19.
g. This reading is from DSS Isaiah.

for fear of the Lord [will come upon them][a],
and the majesty [of the Lord will smite them] when
He arises to cause the earth to tremble.

22 Cease from the human, whose breath is in his nostrils;
for does he merit esteem?

Woe to the Wicked! Hope for the Righteous! (3:1–12)

Isaiah — 3 1 For behold, the Lord, the Lord of Hosts, removes from Jerusalem and from Judah

the supply and the support[b],
the entire supply of bread, and the entire supply of water,

2 warrior and man of war, judge and prophet and wizard and elder, 3 captain of fifty, and notable person, and counselor, and skilled craftsman and caster of spells.

The Lord — 4 "And I will give young people to be their leaders,
and babes will rule over them.

5 And the people will be oppressed—
everyone by another, everyone by a neighbor;

the young person will be disrespectful to the elder,
and the despised against the honored.

6 When a man will take hold of his brother
in the house of his father, saying,

Unnamed individual — 'You have clothing; you will be our leader and let [not][c] this ruin [come] under your hand.'

The Lord — 7 In that day he will say,

Unnamed individual — 'I will not be a healer, for in my house there is neither bread nor clothing. You will not make me a leader of the people.'"

Isaiah — 8 For Jerusalem has stumbled,
and Judah has fallen,

because their [tongues][d] and their deeds are against the Lord,
provoking His glorious eyes.

---

a. Bracketed words in verse 21 are from JST and 2 Nephi 12:21.

b. Isaiah skillfully employs here a feminine form (Hebrew, *mash'enah*) and a masculine form (Hebrew, *mash'en*) of the same word to emphasize the totality of the Lord's removal of food.

c. The words in brackets in verse 6 are from the JST and 2 Nephi 13.

d. From JST and 2 Nephi 13:8.

[9]The look of their faces testifies against them,
and their sin is like Sodom.

They declare it; they do not conceal it.
Woe to their souls!

for they have paid themselves with evil.

[10]Say to the righteous that it is well,
for they will eat the fruit of their deeds.

[11]Woe unto the wicked! It is evil! [For they will perish,][a]
for the dealings of [their hand will be upon them][b].

[12][And][c] my people—children are their oppressors,
and women rule over [you][d].

My people—your guides cause you to err
and confound the way of your paths.

Judgment against the Daughters of Zion (3:13–4:1)

Isaiah [13]The Lord takes His place to plead a cause
and stands to judge peoples.

[14]The Lord enters judgment with the elders
and the leaders of His people;

The Lord "but you, you have consumed the vineyard,
[and][e] the plunder of the poor in your houses.

[15]What do you mean? You crush My people
and grind the faces of the poor?"

Isaiah Declares the Lord, the Lord of Hosts!
[16]And the Lord says,

The Lord "Because the daughters of Zion are haughty,

and they walk with stretched neck and flirtatious eyes,
walking along with strutting steps, walking
with jingling anklets";

Isaiah [17]Therefore the Lord will bring scabs on the
heads of the daughters of Zion,
and the Lord will lay bare their private parts.

---

a. From JST and 2 Nephi 13:11.
b. Bracketed words are from JST.
c. From JST and 2 Nephi 13:12.
d. From JST.
e. The bracketed words are from JST and 2 Nephi 13.

[18] In that day the Lord will take away the glory of the anklets[a], the brow bands, and the crescents, [19] the ear pendants, the bracelets, and the veils, [20] the headdresses, the armlets, the breast-sashes, the receptacles of perfume, and the amulets, [21] the signet-rings, and the nose rings, [22] the festival dresses, the outer garments, the shawls, and the purses, [23] the mirrors, the undergarments, the headbands, and the headcloths.

[24] And it will come to pass, instead of
perfume there will be stench;
and instead of a belt, a rope;
and instead of well-set hair, baldness;
and instead of a rich robe, a girding of sackcloth;
burning instead of beauty[b].

[25] Your men will fall by the sword,
and your warriors in war.

[26] And her {Zion's} entrances will lament and mourn,
and she [will be][c] desolate, [and][d] she will sit on the ground.

4 [1] And in that day, seven women will grasp one man, saying,

Seven women

"We will eat our own bread,
and wear our own apparel;

only let us be called by your name.
Take away our disgrace."

The "Beautiful and Glorious" Lord's Branch (4:2–6)

Isaiah

[2] In that day the Branch of the Lord will
be beautiful and glorious,
and the fruit of the earth will be majestic and glorious
to them that are escaped of Israel.

[3] And it will come to pass, whoever is left in Zion,
and whoever remains in Jerusalem, will be called "Holy,"[e]
everyone that is written for life in Jerusalem.

---

a. A few of the Hebrew words that deal with ornaments, jewelry, and clothing are rare and their precise meaning is uncertain.
b. DSS Isaiah reads "shame instead of beauty."
c. From JST and 2 Nephi 13:26.
d. Bracketed word is from JST.
e. In the Hebrew (*qdsh*), *holy* is sometimes connected to the temple, its ordinances, and God's covenant.

4 The Lord will wash away the filth[a] of the daughters of Zion,
and cleanse the blood from Jerusalem

by the spirit of judgment
and by the spirit of burning.

5 And the LORD will create over the sanctuary of Mount Zion,
and over her solemn assemblies,

a cloud by day
and smoke and the brightness of a flaming fire by night;

for over all the glory [of Zion][b] will be a canopy.
6 It will be as a booth for shade by day from the heat

and for a place of refuge
and for a shelter from the storm and from the rain.

THE SONG OF THE VINEYARD (5:1–7)

Isaiah

5 1 [And then][c], let me sing to my beloved,

"A Song of My Beloved concerning His Vineyard":
My beloved had a vineyard in a fertile hill,

2 and He hoed it and cleared it of stones,
and planted it with a choice vine,

and built a watchtower in it,
and a winepress, too. He hewed in it;

then He waited for it to yield grapes,
but it yielded stinking things.

The LORD

3 "And now, O inhabitant of Jerusalem,
and man of Judah,

judge, please, between Me and My vineyard.

4 What more could have been done to My vineyard
that I have not done for it?

Wherefore, I waited for it to yield grapes;
it yielded stinking things.

5 And now let Me tell you, please, what I will do to My vineyard:

---

a. The Hebrew word *tzo'oh*, translated "filth" literally means "excrement" or "dung."
b. The bracketed words are from JST, 2 Nephi 14:5.
c. The bracketed words are from JST, 2 Nephi 14:5.

I will remove its hedge, and it will burn;
[I will][a] break down its fence, and it will be trampled down;

6 and I will make it wasteland;
it will not be pruned, nor hoed,

but briars and thorns will come up;
I will command the clouds not to rain on it."

Isaiah 7 For the vineyard of the LORD of Hosts is the house of Israel,
and the men of Judah are His delightful plant;

and He waited for justice
and behold, bloodshed!

for righteousness,
but behold a cry of distress!

A LISTING OF SINS AND WOES AGAINST THE WICKED (5:8–25)

Isaiah 8 Woe, who add house to house[b]
until there is no more place,
and you are made to dwell alone in the land.

9 The LORD of Hosts says, in my ears,

The LORD "Surely many houses will be desolate,
[and][c] great and fair [cities][d] without occupants.

10 For ten acres of vineyard will yield nine gallons,
and the seed of the homer will yield a bushel."

Isaiah 11 Woe, who rise early in the morning, to pursue strong drink,
who tarry at twilight, and wine inflame them!

12 And at their banquets they have a lyre, and a harp,
a tambourine and flute, and wine,

but they do not behold the deeds of the LORD,
neither do they see the work of His hands.

13 Therefore my people are exiled, because they lack knowledge;

and their honored men are hungry,
and their masses are parched with thirst.

---

a. Bracketed word is from JST and 2 Nephi 15:5.
b. JST and 2 Nephi 15:8 omit the phrase "and join field to field."
c. Bracketed words from JST and 2 Nephi 15.
d. JST, 2 Nephi 15:9.

[14]Therefore Sheol[a] has enlarged its throat
and opened its mouth without measure;

and into it will descend its splendor, and masses,
and their roar and revelers.

[15]And the human will bow down,
and the man will be humbled,
and the eyes of the lofty will be humbled.

[16]But the Lord of Hosts is exalted in judgment,
and the Holy God shows Himself holy[b] in righteousness.

[17]Then will the lambs feed in their pasture,
and the fatlings and goats will feed among the ruins.

[18]Woe unto them that pull iniquity with cords of falsehood,
and sin with a cart rope, [19]who say,

The wicked "Let Him hurry, let Him hasten His work, that we may see it;
and let the plan of the Holy One of Israel draw
near and come, that we may know it!"

Isaiah [20]Woe unto them that call evil "good"
and good "evil,"

who put darkness for light,
and light for darkness,

who put bitter for sweet,
and sweet for bitter!

[21]Woe unto the wise in their own eyes
and have understanding in their own sight!

[22]Woe unto the mighty ones who drink wine
and the men of strength who mingle strong drink,

[23]who acquit the guilty for a bribe
and deny justice to the righteous.

[24]Therefore, as the tongue of fire devours stubble
and the flame consumes the dry grass,

---

a. *Sheol* is a Hebrew word that denotes the world of spirits. The lexicons state: "the underworld" "whither men descend at death." (*BDB* 982–983); "wasteland, void, underworld" (*HALOT* 4:1369); "netherworld, underworld, abode of the dead." (*DCH* 8:206). Joseph Smith taught, "*Hades*, the Greek, or *Sheol*, the Hebrew, these two significations mean a world of spirits. *Hades*, *Sheol*, paradise, spirits in prison, are all one: it is a world of spirits." (*Teachings*, 310–11).

b For the translational value of this verb, see *Dictionary of Classical Hebrew*, 7:190.

their root will be as stench,
and their blossoms will go up as dust;

because they have rejected the law of the Lord of Hosts,
and the word of the Holy One of Israel, they despised.

25 Therefore is the anger of the Lord
kindled against His people,
and He has stretched forth His hand against
them and has smitten them;

and the mountains did tremble,
and their corpses are like refuse in the streets.

For all this His anger is not turned away,
but His hand is stretched out still.

The Lord Lifts an Ensign to the Nations (5:26–30)

Isaiah

26 And He will lift an ensign to the nations far away,
and He will whistle to those at the ends of the earth;

and behold, they will come quickly, swiftly.

27 None are tired, and none stumble among them;
none will slumber and none will sleep;

none of the belts of their waists come undone,
nor will the straps of their sandals be broken.

28 Their arrows [will be][a] sharp
and all their bows bent,

[and] their horses' hooves are like flint,
and their wheels like a storm;

29 their roaring is like a male lion;
they roar like young lions.

They growl and seize the prey and will carry it off, and none can rescue it.

30 And in that day they will growl against them,
like the growling of the sea;

and if [they][b] look to the land, behold, darkness and distress,
and the light is darkened by the clouds.

---

a. Bracketed words in the verse are from JST and 2 Nephi 15:28.

b. Bracketed word is from JST and 2 Nephi 15:30.

ISAIAH'S VISION OF GOD AND HIS PROPHETIC COMMISSION (6:1–13)

Isaiah 6 [1]In the year of King Uzziah's death, I saw the Lord sitting upon a throne, high and lifted, and the hems of His robe filled the Temple.

[2]Above Him stood seraphs[a], each one had six wings;
with two he {the seraph} covered his face,

and with two he covered his feet,
and with two he flew.

[3]And one called to another and said:

Seraph "Holy, holy, holy is the LORD of Hosts;
the whole earth is full of His glory."

Isaiah [4]And the posts of the thresholds shook at the voice calling out,
and the house was filled with smoke.

[5]Then said I, "Woe is me!
for I am brought to silence,

because I am a man of unclean[b] lips,
and I dwell among a people of unclean lips,

because my eyes have seen the King, the LORD of Hosts."

[6]Then flew one of the seraphs to me, in his hand a glowing coal in tongs that he had taken from the altar;

[7]and he touched my mouth and said,

Seraph "Behold, this has touched your lips,

and your iniquity is removed
and your sin atoned."

Isaiah [8]Also I heard the voice of the Lord, saying:

The LORD "Whom will I send,
and who will go for us?"

Isaiah Then I said, "Here am I; send me." [9]And He said,

---

a. The seraphs are a class of angels that are located in the celestial kingdom. Based on the Hebrew root *saraph* ("to burn"), the term seraph may be translated "burning one" or "bright shining one," referring to the seraphs' glorious condition and location near the Lord's throne.

b. The Hebrew word twice translated "unclean" (*tame'*) in these two lines refers to ceremonial or ritual uncleanness (as per the lexicons).

The Lord “Go, and tell this people,

‘Indeed, hear, but [they][a] will not understand;
and indeed, see, but [they] will not know.’

10 Make the heart of this people fat, and make
their ears heavy, and shut their eyes;
lest they see with their eyes and hear with their
ears and understand with their [hearts][b],

and [be converted][c] and be healed.”

Isaiah 11 Then said I: “How long, O Lord?” And He said:

The Lord “Until the cities lie ruined without inhabitant,
and the houses without a human,
and the land lies wasted and desolate.”

Isaiah 12 And the LORD will remove the human far away, [for there
will be][d] a great forsaking in the land. 13 And yet [there][e] will be
a tenth, and [they] {the tenth} will return. And it will burn like
a terebinth and an oak, which though felled have a trunk that
remains—the holy seed is the trunk.[f]

EPHRAIM AND SYRIA WAR AGAINST JUDAH (7:1–9)

Isaiah 7 1 And it came to pass in the days of Ahaz, the son of Jotham,
the son of Uzziah, king of Judah, that Rezin the king of
Aram, and Pekah the son of Remaliah, king of Israel, went up
to war against Jerusalem, but he could not conquer it. 2 When it
was reported to the house of David, saying,

Unnamed individual “Aram is in league with Ephraim,”

Isaiah then the hearts of Ahaz and his people shook,
just like the trees of the forest shake before the wind.

3 Then the LORD said to Isaiah,

The Lord “Go forth now to meet Ahaz, you and your son Shear-jashub[g],

---

a. Bracketed items are from JST and 2 Nephi 16:9.
b. From JST.
c. From 2 Nephi 16:10.
d. From JST and 2 Nephi 16:12.
e. Bracketed words in verse 13 are from JST and 2 Nephi 16:13.
f. The Hebrew in this verse poses difficulties, making it challenging to translate.
g. The Hebrew name Shear-jashub means “a remnant will return.” In view of the imminent war with Assyria, Shear-jashub was a living symbol that a remnant of

at the end of the aqueduct of the Upper Pool on the road to the Launderer's Field,

4and say to him, 'Be careful, and be quiet;
do not fear, and do not let your heart be faint,

because of these two smoldering sticks of firewood,
because of the raging of Rezin and Aram,
and of the son of Remaliah.

5Because Aram, Ephraim,
and the son of Remaliah have plotted evil against you,' saying,

The Two Kings 6'Let us go up against Judah, and terrify it, and divide it among ourselves, and let us install the son of Tabeal as king over it.'"

Isaiah 7Thus says my Lord, the Lord,

The Lord "It will not happen;
it will not come to pass.

8For the head of Aram is Damascus,
and the head of Damascus is Rezin;

and within sixty-five years Ephraim will be shattered,
that it is no longer a people.

9And the head of Ephraim is Samaria,
and the head of Samaria is Remaliah's son.

If you do not trust,
surely you will not hold firm."

The Sign to Ahaz: The Immanuel Prophecy (7:10–16)

Isaiah 10Again the Lord spoke unto Ahaz, saying,

The Lord 11"Ask a sign of the Lord your God;

let it be in the depths of Sheol[a]
or the heights above."

Isaiah 12But Ahaz said,

Ahaz "I will not ask,
neither will I test the Lord."

Israel would indeed return to its land and God, even though Israel would soon be scattered and for the most part destroyed.

a. On the meaning of the Hebrew word *sheol*, see Isaiah 5:14, footnote a.

Isaiah

[13]And {Isaiah} said, "Hear now, O house of David;

is it a small thing for you to try the patience of men,
but will you try the patience of my God also?

[14]Therefore the Lord Himself will give you a sign—

behold, the virgin[a] will conceive
and will bear a son and call His name Immanuel.[b]

[15]He will eat butter[c] and honey, until he knows to
refuse the evil, and to choose the good.
[16]For before the child knows to refuse the
evil and choose the good,

the land whose two kings you dread will be deserted."

Assyria's Invasion of Judah (7:17–25)

Isaiah (to Ahaz)

[17]The Lord will bring upon you
and upon your people
and upon your father's house

days that have not come,
from the day that Ephraim departed from
Judah—the king of Assyria!

Isaiah

[18]And it will come to pass in that day

that the Lord will whistle for the fly
that is in the end of Egypt[d]
and for the bees that are in the land of Assyria.

[19]And they will come, and all of them rest in the steep ravines,
and in the crevices of the rocks,

and upon all thorn bushes,
and at all the watering places.

[20]In that day the Lord will use the king of Assyria,
hired beyond the river, to shave with a razor:

---

a My translation of virgin is based on the Greek Septuagint, the Vulgate, and the Syriac. Note also that the KJV, ESV, NIV and other translations read "virgin." Compare Proverbs 30:19. The English translation of the Hebrew *'almah* is "marriageable girl" or "young woman." For Mary as a virgin, see Luke 1:27 and 1 Nephi 11:13, 15, 18.

b A Hebrew word, literally, "God with us" (or "God is with us").

c. "Butter" (Hebrew, *chem'ah*) can also be translated "cream" or "sour milk."

d. The JST omits "part of the rivers of."

the head and the hair of the private parts,[a]
and he will also snatch away the beard.

21 And it will come to pass in that day that a man will
keep alive a heifer of the herd and two sheep;
22 and it will come to pass because they will
give an abundance of milk,

he will eat butter;
and everyone who is left in the land will eat butter and honey.

23 And it will come to pass in that day, every place that used to have a thousand vines worth a thousand pieces of silver will be thorns and briars.

24 Men will come there with arrows and bows,
because all the land will become briars and thorns.

25 And all mountains that were once cultivated with the hoe,
one will no longer come there out of fear for briars and thorns,

but they will become places where cattle are turned loose
and where sheep tread.

The Immanuel Prophecy: First Fulfillment (8:1–4)

Isaiah 8 1 And [the word of][b] the Lord said to me,

The Lord "Take for yourself a great tablet and write on it with an ordinary engraving tool: 'Maher-shalal-hash-baz[c].'"

Isaiah 2 And I took faithful witnesses for me—Uriah the priest and Zechariah the son of Jeberechiah. 3 And I drew close to the prophetess, and she conceived and bore a son. Then the Lord said to me,

The Lord "Call his name Maher-shalal-hash-baz. 4 For [behold][d] the child will [not] have knowledge to cry, 'My father and my mother!' [before] the riches of Damascus and the spoil of Samaria will be taken away by the king of Assyria."

---

a. The Hebrew literally reads, "the hair of the feet," where feet is a euphemism for private parts.
b. Bracketed words are from JST and 2 Nephi 18.
c. A prophetic name in Hebrew, which translates into these four words: *speed, spoil, hasten, plunder.*
d. Bracketed words in verse 4 are from JST and 2 Nephi 18:4.

Rejecting the Lord, Who Is the Waters of Shiloah (8:5–10)

Isaiah [5]The Lord spoke unto me again, saying,

The Lord [6]"Because this people refuse the waters
of Shiloah that flow gently,
and rejoice in Rezin and Remaliah's son,

[7]now therefore, behold, the Lord brings
upon them the waters of the river,
mighty and many, even the king of Assyria and all his glory;

and it will come up over all its streambed,
and go over all its banks.

[8]And it will pass over Judah;
it will overflow and go over

until it will reach the neck;
and it will stretch out its wings, filling the breadth
of your land; God is with us! [Immanuel][a].

[9]Band together, O peoples, but you will be broken;
and give ear, all distant parts of the earth;

gird yourselves, but you will be broken;
gird yourselves, but you will be broken.[b]

[10]Counsel together, but it will come to nothing;
speak a word, but it will not stand, for
God is with us! [Immanuel]."

The Lord Is a Temple to the Righteous (8:11–15)

Isaiah [11]For thus the Lord said to me with the grasping of
the hand
and instructed me not to walk in the
way of this people, saying,

---

a. The name Immanuel (Hebrew, "God is with us"), mentioned twice in Isaiah 8 (8:8, 10), is a refrain. It serves to remind the reader of the sign provided to King Ahaz (7:14–16). More importantly, Immanuel is the name of Jesus Christ (see Matthew 1:21–23), who brings spiritual salvation to Israel. In the end, the world's nations and alliances fail because the power of Immanuel exceeds theirs.

b. DSS Isaiah lacks the repeated line, but the repeated words encompass the second line of the parallelism, with the repetition signifying a rhetorical way to emphasize the idea being presented.

The Lord [12]"Do not say, 'Conspiracy,'
whenever this people say, 'Conspiracy';

do not fear what they fear,
neither stand in awe."

Isaiah [13]You will regard the Lord of Hosts as holy; He is your fear,
and you will regard Him with awe. [14]And He will be a Temple,

but He will be a stone of stumbling and a rock
of offense to both the houses of Israel,
a trap and a snare to the inhabitants of Jerusalem.

[15]And many among them will stumble,
and they will fall,

and they will be broken,
and they will be snared,
and they will be captured.

Sealing the Testimony and the Law (8:16–22)

The Lord [16]"Bind up the testimony;
seal the law among My disciples."

Isaiah [17]And I will wait for the Lord, who hides
His face from the house of Jacob,
and I will hope for Him.

[18]Behold, I and the children whom the Lord has given me are
for signs and for wonders in Israel—from the Lord of Hosts,
who resides in Mount Zion. [19]And when they will say unto you,

The wicked "Seek mediums and spiritists,
who whisper and mutter—"

Isaiah Should not a people seek unto their God?
On behalf of the living to [hear from][a] the dead?

[20]To the law and to the testimony; [and][b] if they speak not
according to this word, it is because there is no dawn[c] in them.

[21]And they will pass through it, distressed and hungry;
and it will come to pass that when they become hungry,

---

a. Bracketed words are from JST, 2 Nephi 18:19–20; 19:1.
b. Bracketed word is from JST and 2 Nephi 18:20.
c. Isaiah puts forth *dawn*, not *light* (cf. KJV and other translations). *Dawn* expresses the beginning of light (as in light coming in the morning).

they will become enraged
and curse their king and their gods,

and they will look upward.
22And they will look to the earth

and behold, distress and darkness, uttermost anguish;
and they will be thrust into darkness.

The Messiah—The Son Becomes the New King (9:1–7)

Isaiah

9 1Nevertheless there will be no more gloom for those who
were in anguish. In former times he treated the land of Zeb-
ulun and the land of Naphtali with contempt, but afterward
he will glorify Galilee of the nations, the way of the [Red][a] Sea,
beyond the Jordan.

2The people who are walking in darkness
have seen a great light;
those who are dwelling in the land of the shadow of death,
the light has shined upon them.

3You have increased the nation;
You have magnified the rejoicing.[b]

They rejoice before You as one rejoices at harvest time,
and as they are joyful when dividing the booty,

4because You have shattered the yoke of their burden
and the staff of their shoulder

and the rod of their oppressor, as in the day of Midian[c].

5Because every soldier's boot that tramps with a quake
and every garment rolled in blood

will be for burning,
fuel for the fire.

6Because to us a child is born,
to us a son is given;

and the dominion will be on His shoulder;
and His name will be called
Wonderful Counselor,

---

a. JST and 2 Nephi 2:19.

b. JST, 2 Nephi 19:3 omit "not," for which compare certain medieval Hebrew Bible manuscripts.

c. "As the day of Midian" is not found in 2 Nephi 19:4.

Mighty God,
Everlasting Father,
Prince of Peace.

[7]There is no end to the increase of His dominion and peace

upon the throne of David
and upon His kingdom,

to establish it
and to sustain it

with justice
and with righteousness

from that time on
and forever.

The zeal of the Lord of Hosts will do this.

Judgment against the Northern Kingdom of Israel (9:8–10:4)

Isaiah

[8]The Lord sent [His][a] word unto Jacob,
and it fell upon Israel.

[9]And all the people will know—
Ephraim and the inhabitants of Samaria,

who say in pride
and arrogance of heart,

Samaria's people

[10]"Bricks have fallen, but we will build with hewn stones;
sycamores have been cut down, but we will
replace them with cedars."

Isaiah

[11]Therefore the Lord strengthened Rezin's
adversaries against them
and stirs up their enemies.

[12]Aram on the east,
and the Philistines on the west;

and they will devour Israel with open mouth.

For all this His anger is not turned away,
but His hand is stretched out still.

[13]But the people did not return to Him who smote them,
neither did they seek the Lord of Hosts.

---

a. JST is represented in brackets.

14 Therefore will the Lord cut off from Israel head and tail,
palm branch and reed, in one day.

15 The elder, he is the head;
and a prophet who teaches lies, he is the tail.

16 For those who guide this people cause them to err;
and those who are led by them are confused.

17 Therefore the Lord will not rejoice over their young men,
neither has compassion on their orphans and widows;

for everyone [of them][a] is godless and evil,
and every mouth speaks folly.

For all this His anger is not turned away,
but His hand is stretched out still.
18 For wickedness burns as a fire;
it will devour the briars and thorns,

and will kindle the thickets of the forests,
and they will rise in a column of smoke.

19 Through the wrath of the Lord of Hosts the land grew dark,
and the people will be like fuel for fire.

No man will spare his brother.
20 And he will snatch on the right hand but be hungry,
and he will eat on the left hand, but will not be satisfied;

each will eat the flesh of his own arm.

21 Manasseh, Ephraim; and Ephraim, Manasseh;
together they will be against Judah.

For all this His anger is not turned away,
but His hand is stretched out still.

10 1 Woe to those who decree iniquitous laws
and who constantly write oppressive decrees,

2 to turn away the needy from their legal claim
and to rob justice from the poor of my people,

that widows may be their spoil
and that they may plunder orphans.

3 And what will you do in the day of visitation,
and in the disaster that will come from afar?

a. Word in brackets is from JST.

To whom will you flee for help,
and where will you leave your wealth?

4 Nothing remains but to crouch under the prisoners
or to fall under the slain.

For all this His anger is not turned away,
but His hand is stretched out still.

God Destroys Assyria for Its Wickedness (10:5–19)

The Lord

5 "Woe to Assyria, the rod of My anger,
and the staff of [their][a] fury, it is in their hand.

6 I will send him against a godless nation,
and against the people of My wrath will I command him

to take spoil,
and to seize plunder,
and to make a trampling place, like the mire of the streets.

7 But such is not what he intends,
neither does his heart so think;

because in his heart it is to destroy
and to cut off nations, not a few.
8 For he says,

Assyria's king

'Are not my princes all kings?
9 Was not Calno as Carchemish?
Was not Hamath as Arpad?
Was not Samaria as Damascus?

10 As my hand has founded the kingdoms of the idols,
and whose graven images are greater than
those of Jerusalem and of Samaria?

11 Will I not do to Jerusalem and its idols,
as I have done unto Samaria and its false gods?'"

Isaiah

12 But it will come to pass when the Lord
has completed all His work
upon Mount Zion and upon Jerusalem—

The Lord

"I will punish the fruit of the great heart of the king of Assyria
and the glory of the height of his eyes.
13 For he said,

a. Bracketed items are from 2 Nephi 20.

Assyria's king

'By the strength of my hand and by my wisdom
I have done [these things][a],
for I have understanding;

and I have [moved] the borders of peoples,
and I have plundered their treasures;

like a mighty one,
I have brought down their inhabitants;

14 as one finds a nest,
    my hand has found the wealth of the people,
and as one gathers abandoned eggs,
    I have gathered all the earth;

and there was none that flapped the wing
or opened the mouth and chirped.'"

Isaiah

15 Will the ax boast itself over him who hews with it?
Will the saw make itself greater than him that uses it?

As if a rod can move the man who lifted it,
or a staff lifts the one that is not wood.

16 Therefore the Lord,
the Lord of Hosts,

will send leanness among His fatness;
and instead of His glory,

He will burn with a burning—
like the burning of a fire.

17 And the Light of Israel will become a fire
and their Holy One a flame;

and it [the flame] will burn
and devour his [Assyria's] thorns and briars in one day.

18 And He will consume the glory of His forest
and His fruitful land,

both soul and body;
and it will be as when a sick man wastes away.

19 And the remainder of the trees of His forest will be few,
that a child may write them.

---

a. Bracketed words in verse 13 are from JST and 2 Nephi 20:13.

THE REMNANT OF ISRAEL WILL RETURN (10:20–27)

Isaiah

20 And it will come to pass in that day

that the remnant of Israel
and the survivors of the house of Jacob

will no more again rely on him who smote them
but will in truth rely upon the LORD, the Holy One of Israel.

21 The remnant will return,
[yea][a], the remnant of Jacob, unto the mighty God.

22 For though your people, O Israel, will
be as the sand of the sea,
only a remnant of them will return;

destruction has been decreed, overflowing
with righteousness.
23 For the Lord, the LORD of Hosts is making a complete
destruction, even determined in all the land.

24 Therefore thus says the Lord, the LORD of Hosts,

The LORD

"O My people who dwell in Zion, be not afraid of Assyria;

he will smite you with a rod
and will lift his staff against you, after the manner of Egypt.

25 For in a short time My indignation will cease,
but My anger will be to its destruction."

Isaiah

26 And the LORD of Hosts will lash it with a whip,
like the smiting of Midian at the rock of Oreb;

and He will raise His rod over the sea
after the manner of Egypt.

27 And it will come to pass in that day

He will take away His burden from your shoulder,
and His yoke from off your neck,
and the yoke will be destroyed because of the {anointing} oil.

ASSYRIA MARCHES TO JERUSALEM (10:28–32)

Isaiah

28 He has come to Aiath,
he has passed to Migron;
he stored his supplies at Michmash.

---

a. JST and 2 Nephi 20 in brackets.

[29] They have crossed the pass,
lodging at Geba;

Ramah trembles;
Gibeah of Saul has fled.

[30] Cry out with your voice, O daughter of Gallim;
listen, O Laish; answer her, O Anathoth.

[31] Madmenah flees;
the inhabitants of Gebim have sought refuge.

[32] This very day he stands at Nob;
he will shake his hand against the mountain
of the daughter of Zion,
the hill of Jerusalem.

The Lord Is a Lumberjack (10:33–34)

Isaiah

[33] Behold, the Lord, the Lord of Hosts,

will lop off the boughs with awe-inspiring power;
and the tall ones will be hewn down,
and the lofty will be brought low.

[34] And He will cut down the thickets of the forest with an ax,
and Lebanon will fall by the Mighty One.

The Stump of Jesse Prophecy (11:1–5)

Isaiah

11 [1] And a rod will come forth out of
the Stem {Trunk} of Jesse,
and a branch will grow out of his roots;

[2] And the Spirit of the Lord will rest upon him,
the spirit of wisdom and understanding,

the spirit of counsel and might,
the spirit of knowledge

and fear of the Lord.
[3] And he will delight in the fear of the Lord;

and he will not judge by what he sees with his eyes,
nor decide by what he hears with his ears;

[4] but with righteousness he will judge the poor
and decide with equity for the afflicted of the earth;

but he will smite the earth with the rod of his mouth,
and with the breath of his lips will he slay the wicked.

5 And righteousness will be the sash of his loins
and faithfulness the sash around his waist.

Glorious Conditions of the Millennium (11:6–10)

Isaiah 6 And the wolf will dwell with the lamb,
and the leopard will lie down with the kid;

and the calf and the young lion will graze[a] together,
and a little child will lead them.

7 And the cow and the bear will feed;
their offspring will lie down together;
and the lion will eat straw like an ox.

8 And the nursing babe will play on the hole of the viper,
and the toddler will put his hand on the adder's den.

The Lord 9 "They will not do evil nor destroy in all My holy mountain;"

Isaiah for the earth will be full of the knowledge of the Lord,
as the waters cover the sea.

10 And it will come to pass in that day that the root of Jesse—who stands for an ensign of the people—

to him will the nations seek,
and his place of rest will be glorious.

An Ensign Will Gather Israel (11:11–16)

Isaiah 11 And it will come to pass in that day that the Lord will set His hand again the second time to acquire the remnant of His people

who remain, from Assyria, and from Egypt,
and from Pathros, and from Cush,
and from Elam, and from Shinar, and from
Hamath, and from the islands of the sea.

a. DSS Isaiah reads the verb "to graze" rather than "fatling." "Graze" parallels the verb "lead" in the second line.

12 And He will raise an ensign[a] for the nations,
and will assemble the outcasts of Israel,
and gather the dispersed of Judah
from the four corners of the earth.

13 And the envy of Ephraim will depart,
and those hostile to Judah will be cut off;

Ephraim will not envy Judah,
and Judah will not be hostile toward Ephraim.

14 But they will swoop down the slope of
the Philistines to the west
and plunder the peoples of the east together;

they will stretch out their hands upon Edom and Moab,
and the children of Ammon will be their subjects.

15 And the Lord will completely destroy
the tongue of the Egyptian sea,
and with His scorching wind He will
wave His hand over the river

and will smite it in the seven streams so that men may cross with sandals.

16 And there will be a highway from Assyria for the remnant of
His people, which will be left, as there was for Israel in the day
that they came from the land of Egypt.

Two Hymns of Salvation (12:1–6)

Isaiah **12** 1 And in that day you will say,

Worshipper "O Lord, I will praise You.
Though You were angry with me,
Your anger is turned away,
and You comfort me.
2 Behold, God is my salvation;
I will trust, and not be afraid,
for the Lord, the Lord is my strength and my song;
He has become my salvation.
3 With joy you will draw water out of the springs of salvation."

---

a. Meaning by and with God's authority. The ensign, which may be translated "flag" or "banner," represents the gospel of Jesus Christ (Doctrine and Covenants 45:9; Doctrine and Covenants 105:39).

Isaiah 4 And in that day will you say,

Worshippers "Give praise to the Lord,
call upon His name,

make known His deeds among the people,
call to remembrance that His name is exalted.

5 Sing unto the Lord, for He has done glorious things—
let this be known in all the earth.

6 Cry out[a] and sing gladly, O inhabitant of Zion,
for great in your midst is the Holy One of Israel."

The Lord of Hosts Calls Forth His Hosts (13:1–5)

Isaiah 13 1 A prophecy against[b] Babylon, which Isaiah the son of
Amoz saw.

The Lord 2 "Lift up an ensign on a high mountain,
exalt [My][c] voice unto them,

wave the hand,
that they may enter the gates of the nobles.

3 I have commanded My sanctified ones;
I have also called My mighty ones,

for My anger [is not upon][d] them who rejoice in My majesty."

Isaiah 4 The sound of the multitude in the
mountains, as of a great people,
the sound of the roar of kingdoms,
nations gathering together—

the Lord of Hosts is mustering the host[e] for the battle.

5 They are coming from a distant country,
from the end of the heavens,

---

a. The terms "cry out," "sing gladly," and "inhabitant" are feminine forms in the Hebrew, which means that the final two lines of the second song are directed to a female (possibly referring to Zion?)

b. The Hebrew *masa'* (translated here as "prophecy against") introduces a prophetic judgment against a people or nation (for other examples, see Isaiah 14:28; 15:1; 17:1; 19:1; 21:1; 21:11, 13; 22:1; 23:1; and 30:6).

c. From JST.

d. Bracketed words come from JST, 2 Nephi 23:3.

e. The Hebrew word translated "hosts" (*tzeva'ot*) can also be translated "armies."

[yea][a], the LORD, and the weapons of His indignation,
to destroy the whole land.

JUDGMENT ON BABYLON: THE DAY OF THE LORD WILL COME (13:6–22)

Isaiah

6 Wail, for the day of the LORD is near;
it will come as destruction from the Almighty.

7 Therefore all hands will be feeble;
every human heart will melt.

8 And they will be dismayed,
pangs and agonies will seize them;
they will writhe like a woman in labor.

They will be astonished, one with another;
their faces will be faces of flames.

9 Behold, the day of the LORD comes—
cruel, wrath, and fierce anger—

to make the land desolate;
and He will destroy its sinners from it.

10 For the stars of heaven
and its constellations will not shine their light;

the rising sun will be darkened,
and the moon will not cause its light to shine.

The LORD

11 "And I will punish the world for its evil
and the wicked for their iniquity;

I will cause the arrogance of the proud to cease
and will lay low the haughtiness of the ruthless.

12 I will make men scarcer than fine gold,
and a human, than the pure gold of Ophir.

Therefore, I will make the heavens tremble,
and the earth will shake out of its place,

13 at the wrath of the LORD of Hosts,
and in the day of His fierce anger.

14 Then like a gazelle that is hunted,
or like sheep that no one gathers,

---

a. From JST and 2 Nephi 23:5.

everyone will turn to his own people,
and everyone will flee to his own land.

15 Every one who is [proud][a] will be pierced through;
[yea][b], and everyone who is joined [to the
wicked][c] will fall by the sword.

16 Their children will be dashed to pieces before their eyes;
their houses will be plundered
and their wives ravished.

17 Behold, I am stirring up against them the Medes,

who do not have regard for silver,
nor delight in gold.

18 Their bows will dash the young men to pieces,
and they will have no compassion on the fruit of the womb;
their eyes will not pity children.

19 And Babylon, the beauty of kingdoms,
the glory and pride of the Chaldeans,

will be as when God overthrew Sodom and Gomorrah.

20 It will never be inhabited
or lived in from generation to generation,

nor will the Arabian pitch a tent there,
nor shepherds will make their flocks lie there.

21 But desert animals will lie there,
and their houses will be full of howling creatures,

and ostriches will dwell there,
and wild goats will leap about there.

22 And hyenas will cry in their palaces
and jackals in their palaces of pleasure.

Her {Babylon's} time is about to come,
and its days will not be prolonged.

[For I will destroy her speedily;

yea, for I will be merciful unto My people,
but the wicked will perish.]"[d]

---

a. JST, 2 Nephi 23:15.
b. Bracketed word is from 2 Nephi 23:15.
c. Bracketed words are from JST and 2 Nephi 23:15.
d. JST, 2 Nephi 23:22.

Israel Will Be Gathered, Chosen of God, and Rest from Sorrow (14:1–3)

Isaiah

14 [1]For the Lord will have compassion on Jacob
and will again choose Israel

and give them rest in their land;

and the stranger will be joined with them,
and they will attach themselves to the house of Jacob.

[2]And the people will take them and bring them to their place;
[yea, from far unto the ends of the earth; and they
will return to their lands of promise.][a]

And the house of Israel will possess them
[and the land of the Lord will be][b] for
servants and handmaids;

and they will take them captives [unto
whom][c] they were captives;
and they will rule over their oppressors.

[3]And it will come to pass in [that][d] day,
the Lord will give you[e] rest
from your pain,
and from your turmoil,
and from the difficult labor you were made to serve.

Fall of the King of Babylon (14:4–11)

Isaiah

[4][And it will come to pass in that day][f] that you will take up this proverb against the king of Babylon and say,

Unnamed individual

"How has the oppressor ceased,
the onslaught[g] ceased!"

a. JST, 2 Nephi 24:2.
b. Bracketed words are from JST and 2 Nephi 24:2
c. Bracketed words are from 2 Nephi 24:2.
d. Bracketed word is from JST and 2 Nephi 24:3.
e. Evident in Hebrew but not in the translation is Isaiah's usage of the personal, singular pronouns "you" and "your," meaning that the Lord's promise is personalized to everyone, male and female.
f. From JST, 2 Nephi 24:4.
g. From DSS Isaiah.

Isaiah [5]The LORD has broken the staff of the wicked,
the [scepters][a] of rulers.

[6]He who smote peoples in wrath with unceasing blows,
he that ruled nations in anger with relentless persecution.

[7]The whole earth is at rest, quiet;
they break forth into singing.

[8]Indeed, the cypresses rejoice at you
and also, the cedars of Lebanon:

Trees "Since you were laid down, no woodsman comes up against us."

Isaiah [9]Sheol[b] from beneath trembles to meet you at your coming;
it stirs up the dead spirits for you,

even all the rulers of the earth;
it has raised up all the kings of the nations from their thrones.

[10]All of them will answer and say unto you,

Dead spirits "You also have become weak like us?
You have become like us?"

Isaiah [11]Your pomp is brought down to Sheol;[c]
the sound of your harps [is not heard][d].

Maggots are spread under you,
and worms[e] are your covers.

FALL OF LUCIFER (14:12–23)

Isaiah [12]How you are fallen from heaven, O shining
one[f], son of the morning!
You are cut down to the ground, you who
did weaken the nations!

[13]You have said in your heart,

---

a. Bracketed word is from JST and 2 Nephi 24:9.

b. On the meaning of the Hebrew word *sheol*, see Isaiah 5:14, footnote a.

c. On the meaning of the Hebrew word *sheol*, see Isaiah 5:14, footnote a.

d. Bracketed words are from 2 Nephi 24:11.

e. Isaiah sets forth a wordplay—the Hebrew *tole'ah* means both "worm" and "crimson cloth." The king once used luxurious crimson cloth for this covering, but now worms cover him.

f. The Hebrew word is *helel*, which means "morning-star" or "shining one." Some translations render *helel* as "Lucifer," which comes from the Latin (which literally means "morning star," "light bearer" or similar). Note that Doctrine and Covenants 76:26 also calls Lucifer "a son of the morning." Presumably, Lucifer

Lucifer "I will ascend into heaven;
I will exalt my throne above the stars of God;

I will sit upon the mountain of the divine
    council in the far reaches of the north;

14 I will ascend above the heights of the clouds;
I will make myself like the Most High."

Isaiah 15 But to Sheol[a] you will be brought down,
to the depths of the pit.

16 Those who see you will stare at you
and consider you [and will say:][b]

People "Is this the man who made the earth tremble,
who shook kingdoms,

17 [and][c] who made the world as a wilderness,
and destroyed its cities,
[and] who did not allow his prisoners to go home?"

Isaiah 18 All the kings of the nations—all of them—
lie in glory, each in his own house.

19 But you, you are cast out of your grave
    like an abominable branch,
and the [remnant][d] of those that are slain,
    those pierced by a sword,

who go down to the stones of the pit, like a trampled corpse.
20 You will not be united with them in burial!

Because you have destroyed your land,
and you have slain your people,

the offspring of evildoers will never be named.

21 Prepare slaughter for his children,
for their fathers' [iniquities][e],

lest they possess the earth
and fill the face of the world with cities.

---

had prominence and light in the premortal world, but now he is "cut down" and "fallen from heaven."

a. On the meaning of the Hebrew word *sheol*, see Isaiah 5:14, footnote a.
b. JST, 2 Nephi 24:16.
c. Bracketed words in verse 17 are from JST and 2 Nephi 24:17.
d. Bracketed expression is from JST and 2 Nephi 24:19.
e. Word in brackets is from 2 Nephi 24:21.

The Lord 22“For I will revolt against them,”
Isaiah declares the Lord of Hosts,
The Lord “and I will cut off from Babylon the name,
and remnant, offspring and posterity,”
Isaiah declares the Lord.
The Lord 23“I will make it [Babylon] a possession of the
hedgehog, and pools of water;
and I will sweep it with the broom of destruction,”
Isaiah declares the Lord of Hosts.

God Is in Control of All Nations (14:24–27)

Isaiah 24The Lord of Hosts has sworn, saying,
The Lord “Surely as I have thought, so has it come to pass;
and as I have decided, so will it stand.

25[I will bring][a] the Assyrian in My land,
and on My mountains, I will trample him;

then his yoke will be removed from them,
and his burden will be removed from their shoulders.”

Isaiah 26This is the plan that was planned for the whole earth;
and this is the hand outstretched upon all nations.

27For the Lord of Hosts has decided, and
who will make it invalid?
And His hand is outstretched, and who will turn it back?

Judgment against Philistina (14:28–32)

Isaiah 28This prophecy {against Philistina} came
in the year of King Ahaz’s death.
The Lord 29“Do not rejoice, Philistina, all of you, because
the rod that smote you is broken;

for out of the serpent’s root will come forth an adder,
and its fruit {its offspring} a fiery flying serpent.

30And the firstborn of poor people will find pasture,
and the needy will lie down in safety;

---

a. The bracketed words are from 2 Nephi 24:25.

but I will kill your root with famine,
and your remnant it[a] will slay.

31 Wail, O gate;
cry, O city;

be melted, Philistina, all of you, for smoke comes from
the north, and there is not a straggler in its ranks.

32 What will one say to the envoys of the nations?

'That the LORD has founded Zion,
and in her {Zion} the afflicted of His people will take refuge.'"

A PROPHECY OF DESTRUCTION AGAINST MOAB (15:1–9)

Isaiah

15 1 A prophecy against Moab:

Because in the night Ar of Moab is devastated, destroyed,
Because in the night Kir of Moab is devastated, destroyed,

2 he has gone up to the house {Moab's temple}, and Dibon,
the high places to weep.

Moab wails over Nebo
and over Medeba.

On all their heads is baldness;
every beard is cut off.

3 In their streets they are girded with sackcloth;
on their roofs,
and in their open plazas,

everyone wails,
going down in tears.

4 And Heshbon will cry out, and Elealeh;
their voices will be heard as far as Jahaz.

Therefore, the armed soldiers of Moab will cry aloud;
the soul of each man trembles.

5 My heart cries out for Moab; its fugitives flee
as far as Zoar and Eglath-Shalishiyah,

for at the slope of Luhith, in weeping they go up;
on the way to Horonaim they will lament their destruction.

---

a. DSS Isaiah reads "I will slay."

[6] For the waters of Nimrim will be a wasteland,
for the grass is withered,

the vegetation fails,
there is nothing green.

[7] Therefore the riches that they have made and laid up,
they will carry away to the brook of the willows.

[8] For the cry has reached the borders of Moab;
her {Moab's} wailing as far as Eglaim,
her wailing—to Beer-elim.

The LORD (to Moab)

[9] "For the waters of Dibon will be full of blood,
yet I will bring more upon Dibon,

a lion—to the one who escapes Moab,
and to the remnant of the land."

MOAB SEEKS REFUGE IN JUDAH (16:1–5)

Moabites

16 [1] Send lambs to the ruler of the land
from the rock of the wilderness,
to the mountain of the daughter of Zion.

[2] And it will come to pass, that at the fords
of Arnon the daughters of Moab

will be like a fleeing bird,
cast out of the nest.

[3] Bring forth counsel,
make a decision;

make your shadow
like night during noonday;

hide the refugees;
do not betray the fugitives.

[4] Let my Moabite refugees dwell with you;
be a hiding place to them from the destroyer.

When the oppressor comes to an end,
destruction ceases,
and the trampler is finished from the land;

[5] then the throne will be established with loving-kindness,
and one will sit upon it in truth in the tabernacle of David,

judging, and seeking justice,
and being quick to do righteousness.

LAMENT FOR MOAB (16:6–14)

Leaders/ People of Judah	[6]We have heard of the pride of Moab, of his arrogance and his pride, [for he is very proud][a], and his rage, his lies [and all his evil works]. [7]Therefore Moab will wail for Moab; all of it will wail. For the raisin cakes of Kir-hareseth will you mourn, stricken with grief. [8]For the fields of Heshbon wither, the vines of Sibmah; the lords of the nations have broken down its choice vines, which reach as far as Jazer, and spread to the wilderness; her shoots spread abroad, passing across the sea.
The LORD? Isaiah?	[9]Therefore I weep, as Jazer weeps, for the vines of Sibmah; I water you with my tears, O Heshbon and Elealeh, because over your summer fruits and over your harvest—the shout has fallen. [10]And rejoicing is taken away, and joy from the fruitful field, and no singing gladly in the vineyards, no shout in jubilation. No one treads wine in the wine presses; I have caused the jubilant shout to cease. [11]Therefore my bowels moan like a lyre for Moab and my innermost being for Kir-haresh.
The LORD	[12]"And it will come to pass, when Moab appears at the high place, it will wear itself out; when it comes to its temple to pray, it will be to no avail."
Isaiah	[13]This was the word that the LORD spoke concerning Moab in the past. [14]But now the LORD has spoken, saying,

a. Bracketed words in verse 6 are taken from the JST.

The Lord "Within three years, as a hired worker
considers them, the glory of Moab

with its large population will be lightly esteemed,
and the remnant will be very few and insignificant."

A Prophecy of Judgment against Damascus and Israel (17:1–11)

Isaiah **17** [1]A prophecy against Damascus:

The Lord "Behold, Damascus will cease to be a city,
and it will be a heap of ruins.

[2]The cities of Aroer will be deserted; they
will be a place for flocks,
which will lie down, and none will disturb them.

[3]The fortress will cease from Ephraim,
and the kingdom from Damascus;

and the remnant of Aram
will be like the glory of the children of Israel,"

Isaiah declares the Lord of Hosts.

The Lord [4]"And it will come to pass in that day

that the glory of Jacob will be made thin,
and the fatness of his flesh will become lean.

[5]And it will be like a harvester who gathers standing grain
and reaps ears of grain with his arm;
or it will be like one who gleans ears of grain
in the valley of Rephaim.

[6]Gleanings will be left,
like one who shakes an olive tree,

two or three berries on the topmost bough,
four or five in the branches of a fruitful tree,"

Isaiah declares the Lord God of Israel.

[7]In that day the human will gaze at his Maker,
and his eyes will look to the Holy One of Israel.

[8]And he will not gaze at the altars,
the work of his hands,
neither will look at the Asherim[a] or incense altars,
which his fingers have made.

[9]In that day his stronghold cities will be like the deserted sites of the Hivites and the Amorites,

which they deserted because of the children of Israel,
and there will be desolation.

[10]Because you have forgotten the "God of Your Salvation,"
and the "Rock of Your Stronghold," you have not remembered;

therefore, though you will plant pleasant plants
and sow imported sprigs,

[11]in the day of your planting,
you will make them grow,
and in the morning that you sow,
you will make them blossom,

but the harvest will be a heap
in the day of grief and of incurable pain.

Portrayal of the Downfall of the Nations That Oppress Israel (17:12–14)

Isaiah

[12]Woe to the multitude of many people,
who are turbulent like the turbulence of the seas;
O the roar of nations,
the roar like the roar of mighty waters!

[13]The nations roar like the roar of many waters,
but He will rebuke them,

and they will flee far away
and will be chased

like the chaff of the mountains before the wind
and like a tumbleweed before the whirlwind.

[14]And behold, in the evening—terror!
And before morning—they are gone!

a. This is a Hebrew plural word, which refers to Canaanite goddesses (idols) or the cultic poles (or trees) that represented them. The singular form is *Asherah*.

God's covenant people

"Such is the portion of those who loot us,
and the lot of those who plunder us."

The Lord's Messengers Take the Gospel to the World (18:1–7)

Isaiah

18 1 Ah, the land whirring with wings, which is beyond
the rivers of Cush, 2 that sends ambassadors by the sea
in vessels of reeds upon the waters. Go, swift messengers, to
a nation tall and smooth-skinned, to a people feared far and
wide, a mighty and conquering nation, whose land the rivers
have divided.[a]

3 All inhabitants of the world
and dwellers on the earth,

when an ensign is raised on the mountains, you will see;
when a trumpet is blown, you will hear.

4 For thus says the Lord to me,

The Lord

"I will be still,
and I will look from My dwelling place,

like shimmering heat in the light
and like a cloud of dew in the heat of harvest."

Isaiah

5 For before the harvest,
after the budding and the blossoms become ripening grapes,

He will cut off the shoots with pruning hooks
and cut down and take away the spreading branches.

6 They will be left together for the mountain birds of prey
and for the wild animals of the earth,

and the birds of prey will summer on them,
and all the wild animals of the earth will winter on them.

7 At that time a gift will be brought to the Lord of
Hosts, from a people tall and smooth-skinned,
and from a people feared far and wide,
a mighty and conquering nation, whose
land the rivers have divided,

to the place of the name of the Lord of Hosts—
Mount Zion!

---

a. The verse presents difficult Hebrew expressions, which makes a flawless translation impossible.

The Lord Smites Egypt and Later Heals It (19:1–25)

Isaiah

19 1 A prophecy against Egypt:
Behold, the Lord is riding on a swift
cloud and is coming to Egypt,

and the idols of Egypt will tremble at His presence,
and the heart of Egypt will melt within it.

The Lord

2 "And I will provoke Egyptian against Egyptian,
and they will fight, everyone against his brother,

and everyone against his neighbor, city against city,
kingdom against kingdom.

3 And the spirit of the Egyptians will be emptied from within,
and I will confound their plans,

and they will seek the idols
and the spirits of the dead
and the mediums and spiritists.

4 And I will deliver the Egyptians into the cruel masters,
and a mighty king will rule over them,"

Isaiah

declares the Lord, the Lord of Hosts.

The Lord

5 And the waters of the sea will dry up,
and the river will be parched and dry.

6 And the rivers will become foul,
and the branches of Egypt's Nile will diminish and dry up.

The reeds and rushes will wither;
7 the reeds along the Nile, on the banks of the Nile,

everything that is sown by the Nile will dry up,
be driven away and be no more.

8 And the fishermen will mourn,
and all who cast fishhook into the Nile will lament,
and those who spread fishing nets upon
the waters will grieve.

9 Those who work with flax that is combed will be ashamed,
and the weavers will turn pale.

10 And its foundations will be crushed,
and all wage earners will despair.

11 Surely the officials of Zoan are fools;
the wise counselors of Pharaoh give absurd council,

How can one say to Pharaoh,

Unnamed individual

"I am descended from wise men;
I am descended from ancient kings?"

Isaiah

12 Where are they?
Where are your wise men?

Let them tell you now
and make known what the Lord of Hosts
has planned against Egypt.

13 The officers of Zoan have become fools;
the officers of Memphis are deceived.

They have caused Egypt to err,
the cornerstone of its tribes.

14 The Lord has mingled within it a spirit of confusion,

and they have caused Egypt to stagger in all its works,
as a drunk staggers in his vomit.

15 And there will be nothing for Egypt
that head or tail, palm branch or reed, may do.

16 In that day the Egyptians will be like women,
and will tremble and fear

because of the uplifted hand of the Lord of Hosts,
which He lifts over it.

17 And the land of Judah will be a terror to Egypt,
and it will fear whenever anyone mentions it,

because of what the Lord of Hosts is planning against it.
18 In that day there will be five cities in the land

of Egypt speaking the language of Canaan
and swearing to the Lord of Hosts.

Unnamed individuals

"The City of the Sun,"[a]

Isaiah

it will be said of one of them.

19 In that day will there be

an altar to the Lord in the midst of the land of Egypt
and a pillar to the Lord at its border.

---

a. This reading is from DSS Isaiah.

[20]And it will be for a sign and for a witness unto the
Lord of Hosts in the land of Egypt, for they will
cry unto the Lord because of oppressors,

and He will send them the Savior,
and the Defender, and He will deliver them.

[21]And the Lord will be known to the Egyptians,
and the Egyptians will know the Lord in that day,

and they will worship with sacrifice and offerings,
and they will vow a vow unto the Lord and perform it.

[22]And the Lord will smite Egypt;
He will smite and heal it,

and they will return to the Lord,
and He will heed their supplications, and He will heal them.

[23]In that day there will be a highway from Egypt to Assyria,
and Assyria will come into Egypt,

and Egypt into Assyria,
and Egypt will worship with Assyria.

[24]In that day will Israel be the third with
Egypt and with Assyria,
a blessing in the midst of the earth.

[25]The Lord of Hosts will bless them, saying,

The Lord "Blessed is Egypt, My people,

and Assyria, the work of My hands,
and Israel, My inheritance."

Conquest of Egypt and Cush: Isaiah's Dramatization (20:1–6)

Isaiah 20 [1]In the year that Tartan—sent by Sargon, the king of
Assyria—came to Ashdod and fought against it and
captured it, [2]at that time the Lord spoke by Isaiah the son of
Amoz, saying,

The Lord "Go and remove the sackcloth from your loins
and take off the sandals from your feet."

Isaiah And he did so, walking naked and
barefoot. [3]And the Lord said,

The Lord "Just as My servant Isaiah walked naked and barefoot three
years as a sign and a wonder for Egypt and Cush, [4]so will the
king of Assyria lead away the captives of Egypt, and the exiles

of Cush, young and old, naked and barefoot, even with their
buttocks uncovered—the nakedness of Egypt. 5 Then those
who made Cush their hope, and Egypt their glory, will be
dismayed and ashamed. 6 And the inhabitants of this coast
will say in that day,

Inhabitants of Judah

'Behold, thus was our hope, and to whom we fled for help to be delivered from the king of Assyria, how will we escape?'"

A Prophecy of Judgment against Babylon (21:1–10)

Isaiah

21 1 A prophecy against the desert of the sea.

As whirlwinds in the south sweep through,
so, it comes from the wilderness, from a terrible land.

2 A harsh vision was declared unto me:

Unnamed individual

"The traitor is betraying,
and the destroyer is destroying."

Military leader

"Go up, O Elam;
lay siege, O Media!"

Unnamed individual

"I have caused all of the sighing to cease."

Isaiah

3 Therefore my loins are filled with anguish;
pangs have seized me,
as the pangs of a woman who is in labor.

I was bowed down at what I heard;
I was dismayed at what I saw.

4 My heart went astray, shuddering fell upon me;
the twilight that I desired put me to trembling.

5 Prepare the table, watch in the watchtower,
eat, drink,

arise, O you officers.
Anoint the shield.

6 For thus the Lord said unto me,

The Lord

"Go, post a watchman;
let him declare what he sees."

Isaiah

7 And he saw chariots, with teams of horses,
riders on donkeys, riders on camels;

and he paid attention,
great attention.

8 And the seer[a] cried,

Seer — "My Lord,

I stand continually upon the watchtower all day,
and I am stationed at my post all night.

9 And, behold, this is coming: a chariot of a man,
a pair of horsemen."

Isaiah — And he answered and said,

Unnamed messenger — "Babylon is fallen, is fallen;
and all the graven images of its gods he
has shattered to the ground."

The Lord — 10 "O my threshed!
O child of my threshing floor!"

Isaiah — I have declared that which I have heard from
the Lord of Hosts, the God of Israel.

A Prophecy of Judgment against Dumah (21:11–12)

Isaiah — 11 A prophecy against Dumah:
One calls to me from Seir,

Individual from Seir — "Watchman, what of the night?
Watchman, what of the night?"

Isaiah — 12 The watchman said,

Watchman — "The morning is coming,
and also, the night;

if you will inquire,
then inquire,

return,
come."

A Prophecy of Judgment against Arabia (21:13–17)

Isaiah — 13 A prophecy against Arabia:

You will lodge in the forest in Arabia, O caravans of Dedanim.

---

a. DSS Isaiah correctly attests "seer" rather than "lion."

14 Bring water to meet the thirsty,
O inhabitants of the land of Tema;
go up to the refugee with bread.

15 Because they fled from swords,
from the drawn sword,

and from the bent bow,
and from the heat of battle.

16 For thus the Lord said unto me,

The Lord

"Within a year, as a hired worker would count it, all the
glory of Kedar will come to an end, 17 and the remnant of the
number of archers, the mighty men of Kedar, will be few."

Isaiah

For the Lord God of Israel has spoken it.

A Prophecy of Judgment against Jerusalem (22:1–14)

Isaiah to Jerusalem

22 1 A prophecy against the valley of vision:
What has happened to you,
that all of you have gone up to the housetops?

2 Noises! O city full of commotion,
a jubilant town.

Your slain are not slain with the sword,
nor are they dead from war.

3 All your leaders have fled together,
but they were captured without a bow;
all who could be found have been captured,
though together they had fled far away.

4 Therefore I said,

Isaiah

"Look away from me; let me weep bitterly.
Do not try to comfort me, because of the
destruction of the daughter of my people."

Isaiah to Jerusalem's inhabitants

5 For it is a day of tumult and of trampling
and confusion by the Lord, the Lord of
Hosts in the valley of vision,

battering down of walls
and of crying to the mountain.

6 And Elam bare the quiver in chariots of horsemen,
and Kir uncovered the shield.

[7]And it came to pass that your choicest
valleys were filled with chariots,
and the horsemen took their stand at the gate.

[8]And the covering of Judah was exposed,
but you looked in that day to the weapons
of the House of the Forest.

[9]And you saw that there were many
breaches in the City of David,
and you stored up the water of the lower pool.

[10]And you counted the houses of Jerusalem
and broke down houses in order to strengthen the wall.

[11]Between the two walls you made a reservoir
for the water of the old pool,

but you did not look to the One who made it,
nor did you see the One who fashioned it long ago.

[12]And in that day the Lord,
the Lord of Hosts,

called for weeping,
and mourning,
and shaving the head,
and girding with sackcloth.

[13]But behold, exultation
and rejoicing,

slaying oxen,
and slaughtering sheep,

eating flesh,
and drinking wine;

Reveler "Eat and drink,
for tomorrow we die."

Isaiah [14]And the Lord of Hosts has revealed in my ears,

The Lord "Surely this iniquity will not be atoned for you until you die,"

Isaiah says the Lord, the Lord of Hosts.

Judgment upon Shebna and Blessings upon Eliakim (22:15–25)

Isaiah [15]Thus says the Lord,
the Lord of Hosts,

The Lord "Go, come to this administrator, to Shebna,
who is over the house:

[16]'What have you here,
and whom have you here,

that you have hewn a tomb here for yourself?'"

Isaiah He hews out a tomb on the height!
He cuts out in the rock a dwelling for himself!

[17]Behold, the Lord will assuredly hurl you away,
O mighty man, and firmly seize you.

[18]He will certainly whirl you round
and round like a ball to a large country;

there you will die,
and there your glorious chariots will be the
shame of your master's house.

The Lord [19]"And I will thrust you from your station,
and from your position he will cast you."

[20]And it will come to pass in that day that I will call
my servant Eliakim, the son of Hilkiah,

[21]and I will clothe him with your robe,
and your sash, I will bind on him,

and I will commit your rule into his hand,
and he will be a father to the inhabitants of Jerusalem
and to the house of Judah.

[22]And I will place on his shoulder the
key of the house of David;

and he will open, and no one will shut;
and he will shut, and no one will open.

[23]And I will fasten him as a nail in a sure place;
and he will be a throne of glory to his father's house.

[24]And they will hang upon him all the
glory of his father's house,
the offspring and the issue,

all small vessels,
from the bowls, even to all jars."

Isaiah [25]In that day, declares the Lord of Hosts,

The Lord “the nail that is fastened in the sure place will be removed
and be cut down and fall;
and the burden that was upon it will be cut off.”

Isaiah For the Lord has spoken.

The Lament of the Destruction of Tyre and Sidon (23:1–18)

Isaiah 23 1 A prophecy against Tyre:
Wail, O ships of Tarshish, for it is destroyed,
without house or harbor.
It is revealed to them from the land of Kittim.

2 Be silent, O inhabitants of the coast,
O merchants of Sidon,

whose messengers crossed the sea
3 and were on the many waters.

The grain of Sihor, the harvest of the Nile, was its revenue,
and she was the trade center of the nations.

4 Be ashamed, O Sidon, for the sea has said,
the stronghold of the sea, saying,

Tyre “I have not labored with child,
nor have I given birth;

I have not raised young men,
nor have I brought up virgin girls.”

Isaiah 5 When the report reached Egypt,
they experience labor pains over the report concerning Tyre.

6 Cross over to Tarshish.
Wail, O inhabitants of the coast.

Unnamed individual 7 “Is this your exultant {city}, founded in days of old?
On whose feet you were carried to settle far away?

8 Who has planned this against Tyre,
the one who bestows crowns,

whose merchants were princes,
whose traders were the honored of the earth?”

Isaiah

[9]The Lord of Hosts has planned it,
to defile the pride of all beauty,
to dishonor all the honored of the earth.

[10]Pass through your land[a] like the Nile, O daughter
of Tarshish; there is no longer a harbor.

[11]He {God} stretched out His hand over the sea.
He made the kingdoms tremble.
The Lord has commanded to Canaan,
to destroy its strongholds.

[12]And He said,

The Lord

"You will no longer exult, O oppressed virgin,
daughter of Sidon.

Arise, cross over to Kittim;
even there, you will have no rest.

[13]Behold, the land of the Chaldeans.
This is the people that is not.

Assyria destined it for desert-beasts.
They erected their siege-towers.
They stripped its palaces.
They made it a ruin.

[14]Wail, O ships of Tarshish, for your stronghold is destroyed."

Isaiah

[15]And it will come to pass, in that day, Tyre will be forgotten for seventy years, the lifetime of one king. At the end of seventy years, it will be with Tyre as the song about the harlot:

Unnamed individual

[16]"Take a harp,
go about the city, O forgotten harlot;

play skillfully,
multiply songs, so that you will be remembered."

Isaiah

[17]And it will come to pass, at the end of seventy years, the Lord will visit Tyre, and it will return to its hire and will play the harlot with all the kingdoms of the world upon the face of the earth. [18]Its merchandise and its hire will be holiness to the Lord; it will not be stored nor hoarded. But its merchandise will be for abundant food and fine clothing for those who dwell before the Lord.

---

a. DSS Isaiah has "Cultivate your land."

The World Changes the Ordinance and Breaks the Covenant (24:1–12)

Isaiah

24 [1]Behold, the Lord is emptying the earth
and making it waste,
and He twists its surface
and scatters its inhabitants.

[2]And it will be the same for the people, as it is with the priest;
the slave, as it is with his master;

the maid, as it is with her mistress;
the buyer, as it is with the seller;

the borrower, as it is with the lender;
the debtor, as it is with the creditor.

[3]The earth will be completely emptied
and totally plundered, for the Lord has spoken this word.

[4]The earth mourns, withers;
the world languishes, withers.
The haughty of the people of the earth languish.

[5]The earth is polluted beneath its inhabitants

for they have transgressed the laws,
they have changed the ordinance[a],
they have broken the everlasting covenant.

[6]Therefore, a curse consumes the earth,
and its inhabitants must bear their guilt.

Therefore, the inhabitants of the earth are burned,
and few men remain.

[7]The new wine mourns,
the vine languishes;

all who have rejoicing hearts sigh,
[8]the exultation of tambourines has ceased;
the roar of the jubilant has stopped,
the exultation of the harp has ceased.

[9]No more do they drink wine with song;
strong drink is bitter to those who drink it.

[10]The town of chaos is broken down.
Every house is shut, no one can enter.

---

a. "Ordinance" (Hebrew, *choq*) comes from the root *chaqaq*, meaning to "carve or engrave."

[11]In the streets, there is an outcry over the wine.
All rejoicing has grown dark;
the exultation of the earth is banished.

[12]Desolation remains in the city;
the gates are crushed to ruins.

A Righteous Remnant Sings Gladly (24:13–16a)

Isaiah

[13]For thus it will be in the midst of the earth,
among the peoples,

as when an olive tree is beaten,
as the gleanings after the grape harvest.

[14]They lift their voices;
they sing gladly.

Because of the majesty of the Lord,
they cry out from the west.

[15]Therefore, glorify the Lord in the region of light,
in the coastlands of the sea—

the name of the Lord,
the God of Israel.

[16]From the ends of the earth, we hear songs:

God's covenant people

"Glory[a] to the Righteous One!"

The Earth Reacts to Its Inhabitants' Iniquities (24:16b–23)

Isaiah

[16]But I say, "I waste away,
I waste away; woe is me!

For the traitors have betrayed;[b]
with betrayal the traitors have betrayed.

[17]O inhabitant of the earth—dread, and the pit,
and the snare are upon you.

---

a. "Glory" (Hebrew, *tzvi*) can also be translated as "beauty," meaning the Righteous One also has beauty.

b. Isaiah uses a clever wordplay, wherein he repeats the root Hebrew term *bagad* ("betray") five times. His wordplay is largely lost in the English translation, but I have tried to provide a literal translation (although it is somewhat awkward).

18And it will come to pass,
he who flees from the noise of the dread will fall into the pit,
and he who climbs out of the pit will be caught in the snare,

for the windows of heaven are opened,
and the foundations of the earth tremble.

19The earth is completely broken,
the earth is altogether split,
the earth totally shakes.

20The earth[a] will reel to and fro like a drunkard;
it sways like a hut.

Its iniquity will weigh it down, that it will fall
and will not rise again.

21And on that day the Lord will punish
the host of high ones above
and the kings of the earth below.

22And they will be gathered together as prisoners in a pit,
and they will be shut up in prison and after
many days they will be visited.
23The moon will be confounded
and the sun ashamed.

For the Lord of Hosts will reign on Mount Zion
and in Jerusalem, in glory, and before His elders."

Praise to God; Triumph over the Wicked (25:1–5)

Isaiah

25 1O Lord,
You are my God.

I will exalt You;
I will praise Your name,

because You have done wonderful things,
plans of old, in perfect faithfulness.

2For You have made a city into a heap,
a fortified town into a ruin,

---

a. Note that Isaiah portrays the earth as a person, specifically as a female (the Hebrew uses feminine grammatical forms when it refers to the earth; these forms are lost in the translation) to indicate the anguish of the earth as she deals with her inhabitants' evil conduct.

a palace of foreigners, a city no more;
it will never be rebuilt.

3 Therefore mighty people will honor You;
a town of ruthless nations will fear You.

4 For You have been a stronghold to the poor,
a stronghold to the needy in their distress,

a place of refuge from the storm,
shade from the heat,

when the wind of the ruthless is like a storm against a wall,
5 like heat on parched ground.

You will subdue the roar of foreigners;
as heat is diminished by the shade of a cloud,
the song of the ruthless will be stilled.

THE LORD PREPARES A FEAST FOR THE RIGHTEOUS (25:6–12)

Isaiah

6 On this mountain, the LORD of Hosts will make
a feast of fat things for all people, a feast of wines on the lees,
fat things full of marrow, well-refined, wines on the lees.

7 And on this mountain He will swallow up
the covering that covers all peoples,
and the veil that is spread over all nations.

8 He will swallow up death forever, and the Lord,
the LORD will wipe away the tears from all faces,

and He will remove the disgrace of His
people from all the earth,
for the LORD has spoken.

9 And it will be said on that day,

God's covenant people

"Behold, this is our God; we have waited
for Him, that He might save us.
This is the LORD; we have waited for Him.

Let us be joyful,
and let us rejoice in His salvation.

10 For the hand of the LORD will rest on this mountain.

And Moab will be trodden down under Him,
as straw is trodden down in a dung-pit.

[11]And {Moab} will spread out its hands in
the midst of it {the dung-pit},
as a swimmer spreads his hands to swim,

but He {the Lord} will lay low their pride
together with the skill of His hands.
[12]And their high, fortified walls He will bring down.

He will lay low;
He will cast to the ground, even to dust."

A Song about a "Strong City" Versus the "Lofty Town" (26:1–6)

Isaiah

26 [1]In that day this song will be sung in the land of Judah:

God's covenant people

"We have a strong city;
He {the Lord} makes salvation as its walls and its rampart.

[2]Open Your[a] gates that the righteous nation,
which keeps faith, may enter in.

[3]You will keep those in perfect peace,
whose mind rests on You, because they trust in You.

[4]Trust in the Lord forever and ever,
because the Lord, the Lord is the Everlasting Rock.

For He has brought low those who dwell on high;
a lofty town, He lays it low.

[5]He lays it low, to the ground;
He casts it to the dust.

[6]The foot tramples it, the feet of the poor,
the footsteps of the needy."

A Prayer about the Lord's Judgments (26:7–18)

God's covenant people

[7]"The way of the righteous, it is a level path;
it is level, the path of the righteous.

[8]Yea, O Lord, we wait in the path of Your judgments;
{our} soul's desire are for Your name and Your remembrance.

---

a. DSS Isaiah has the personal pronoun "Your," which refers to the Lord.

Unnamed individual

[9]'With my soul, I long for You in the night;
yea, with my spirit within me, I seek You early.

For when Your judgments are on the earth,
the inhabitants of the world learn righteousness.

[10]Though grace is shown to the wicked,
he does not learn righteousness.
In the land of uprightness, he deals with corruption
and does not see the majesty of the LORD.

[11]O LORD, Your hand is lifted up, but they will not see;
but let them see and be ashamed

for the envy of the people;
yea, let the fire for Your adversaries consume them.'

God's covenant people

[12]O LORD, You will offer peace for us,
for You have performed all our works for us.

[13]O LORD, our God, lords besides You have ruled over us;
in You alone, we bring to remembrance Your name.

[14]They are dead; they live no more.
Their spirits do not arise.

Therefore, You have punished them,
and You have destroyed them
and have made all memory of them to perish.

[15]You have increased the nation, O LORD;
You have increased the nation; You are glorified.
You have extended all the boundaries of the land.

[16]O LORD, they sought You in distress;
they poured out a whisper when Your
chastening was upon them.

[17]Like a woman with child when she is about to give birth,
who writhes and cries out in her pangs,

so were we, because of You,
O LORD.

[18]We were with child;
we writhed. It is as though we have given birth to wind.
We have not brought salvation to the earth,
and the inhabitants of the world have not come to life."

The Lord Responds to Israel's Prayer and Promises the Resurrection (26:19–21)

The Lord 19"Your dead will live;
their bodies will rise.

Awake and sing gladly, O you who dwell in the dust.
For your dew is a dew of lights[a] and the
earth will cast out the dead.

20Go, My people, enter your chambers and
shut your doors behind you;
hide for a little moment until the wrath has passed over."

Isaiah 21For behold, the Lord is coming forth out of His place
to punish the inhabitants of the earth for their iniquity

and the earth will reveal the bloodshed upon it
and will no longer cover its slain.

Israel Will Be Gathered in the Last Days (27:1–13)

Isaiah 27 1In that day the Lord will punish—
with His hard, great, and strong sword—

Leviathan, a fleeing serpent,
Leviathan, a coiling serpent, and He will
slay the monster that is in the sea.

2In that day, delightful vineyard, sing to it!

The Lord 3"I, the Lord, am its keeper;
moment by moment I water it.

I keep it night and day so that no harm comes to it.
4I have no wrath.

Who will give Me thorns and briars?
I will march against them in battle;
I will burn them up together;

5but if they lay hold of My strength,
he will make peace with Me;
peace he will make with Me."

---

a. "Dew of lights," a literal translation from the Hebrew *tal 'orot*, is a poetic expression that beautifully compares the glistening light on the morning dew to the Resurrection.

Isaiah

[6]In days to come, Jacob will take root;
Israel will blossom and flower,
and they will fill the face of the world with fruit.

[7]Has He smote {Israel} as He smote those who smote {Israel}?
Or has {Israel} been slain as its slayers were slain?

[8]By exact measure, by sending {Israel}
away, You contended with it.
He removed it with His hard wind, in the day of the east wind.

[9]Therefore by this will the iniquity of Jacob be atoned for,
and this will be the full fruit of the removal of his sin;

when He makes all the stones of the altar,
like chalkstones crushed to pieces,
no Asherim or incense altars will remain standing.

[10]For a fortified city is solitary,
a deserted and forsaken habitation, like the wilderness;

a calf grazes there, and there it lies down
and consumes its branches.

[11]When its branches are dry, they are broken.
Women come, light fires with them.
For they are a people without understanding;

therefore, their Maker will not have compassion on them;
their Fashioner will show them no favor.

[12]And in that day, the Lord will thresh out the
grain from the river to the wadi of Egypt,
and you will be gathered one by one, O people of Israel.

[13]And in that day a great ram's horn will be blown,
and those lost in the land of Assyria
and those scattered in the land of Egypt will come,

and they will worship the Lord
on the holy mountain, in Jerusalem.

Isaiah Prophesies of the Destruction of Ephraim (28:1–8)

Isaiah

28 [1]Woe crown of the pride of the drunkards of Ephraim,
and the fading flower of its glorious beauty,

which is at the head of a fertile valley,
to those who are overcome with wine.

[2]Behold, the Lord has one who is mighty and strong,
like a hailstorm,
a destroying tempest,
like a storm of mighty overflowing waters;
and with a hand, he casts down to the earth.

[3]The crown of the pride of the drunkards of
Ephraim will be trampled underfoot.
[4]And the fading flower of its glorious beauty,
which is at the head of a fertile valley,

will be like the early ripe fig before the summer,
which one sees, and as soon as it is in his palm, he swallows it.

[5]In that day the Lord of Hosts will be a crown of beauty
and a beautiful diadem to the remnant of His people

[6]and a spirit of judgment to him who sits in judgment
and strength to those who fend off battle at the gate.

[7]And also these reel with wine
and stagger with strong drink;

priest and prophet reel with strong drink;
they are confused with wine;
they stagger with strong drink.

They reel in their visions;
they stumble in their decisions,

[8]for all the tables are full of vomit,
filth, with no space left.

Individuals Learn Doctrine Line upon Line (28:9–13)

Isaiah?

[9]To whom will He teach knowledge?
Whom will He cause to understand the message?

Those who are weaned from milk;
those who are taken from breasts.

[10]For it is precept[a] upon precept,
precept upon precept,

line upon line,
line upon line,

a. "Precept" can also be translated "command" (from the Hebrew *tzwh*), hence reading "command upon command, command upon command."

here a little,
there a little.

[11]For with stammering lips
and with another tongue He will speak to this people,

[12]to those whom He has said,

The Lord "This is the rest: give rest to the weary"
and "this is the resting place,"

Isaiah but they are not willing to hear.

[13]And the word of the Lord will be to them
precept upon precept,
precept upon precept,

line upon line,
line upon line,

here a little,
there a little,

so that they may go.
But they stumbled backward

and were broken
and snared and captured.

The Overflowing Scourge (28:14–22)

Isaiah [14]Therefore, hear the word of the Lord, men of scorning,
who rule this people who are in Jerusalem.

[15]Because you have said,

Men of scorning "We have made a covenant with death,
and with Sheol,[a] we made an agreement.

When an overflowing scourge passes through,
it will not come to us,

for we have made a lie our place of refuge,
and we have taken shelter in falsehood."

Isaiah [16]Therefore, thus the Lord, the Lord says,

The Lord "Behold I am laying a stone in Zion,
a tested stone,

a precious cornerstone,
a sure foundation. He who believes will not have to move.

a. On the meaning of the Hebrew word *sheol*, see Isaiah 5:14, footnote a.

[17]And I will make judgment the measuring line
and righteousness the plumb line.

And hail will sweep away a refuge of lies,
and waters will flood a shelter.

[18]Then your covenant with death will be annulled
and your agreement with Sheol[a] will not stand;

when the overflowing scourge passes through,
then you will be beaten down.

[19]As often as it passes through it will take you,
because morning after morning,
by day and by night, it will pass through, and it will
be sheer terror to understand the report."

Isaiah

[20]For the bed is too short for one to stretch oneself on it,
and the blanket too narrow to wrap oneself in it.

[21]For like Mount Perazim the Lord will rise;
like the valley of Gibeon, He will quake,

to do His work, His strange work,
and to perform His act, His strange act.

[22]And now, do not scoff,
lest your bonds be made strong,

because I have heard from the Lord, the Lord of Hosts,
a decree of destruction upon the whole earth.

Parable of the Farmer (28:23–29)

Isaiah

[23]Give ear, and hear my voice;
hearken, and hear my speech.

[24]Does the plowman plow all day,
breaking up and harrowing his ground for sowing?

[25]Once he has leveled its surface,
does he not scatter dill and cast cumin?

And he puts wheat in rows,
and barley in its proper place,
and spelt around the border?

[26]For He {God} teaches him judgment;
his God instructs him.

---

a. On the meaning of the Hebrew word *sheol*, see Isaiah 5:14, footnote a.

27 For dill is not threshed with a threshing sledge,
nor is a cartwheel rolled over cumin,

but dill is beaten out with a staff
and cumin with a rod.

28 Grain is crushed, but the thresher does not thresh it forever.
When he drives his cartwheel with his horses,
he does not crush it.

29 This also goes forth from the Lord of Hosts—

He provides wonderful counsel;
He magnifies wisdom.

Jerusalem to Be Brought Down by the Lord (29:1–10)

Isaiah 29 1 Woe![a] O Ariel, Ariel,
the town where David encamped.

Add year upon year;
let the festivals go through the cycle.

The Lord 2 And I will cause distress to Ariel;
and there will be mourning and sorrow!"

Isaiah [For thus has the Lord said unto me][b],

The Lord "It will be unto Ariel,
3 [that][c] I [the Lord] will camp against [her] round about;
and besiege [her] with a mound
and I will raise siege works against [her].

4 And [she][d] will be brought low and speak from the earth;
and [her] speech will be low out of the dust,

and [her] voice will be like a spirit of
the dead[e], from the earth,
and [she] will whisper from the dust.

---

a. Distress will come to Jerusalem's inhabitants because of God's forthcoming judgments. *Ariel, Ariel.* A name of Jerusalem, which is translated "lion of God," "lioness of God," or "altar-hearth" of God. The lion is a symbol of Judah (Genesis 49:9).

b. Words in brackets are from JST.

c. Bracketed words in verse 3 are from JST.

d. Bracketed words in verse 4 are from JST.

e. The word translated "spirit of the dead" (Hebrew *'ov*) is difficult to translate. The lexicons present various translations, including "skin-bottle," "necromancer," "ghost," "medium," and "spirit of the dead." In my view, "spirit of the dead" makes

[5]And the multitude of [her][a] strangers
will become like fine dust
and the multitude of the ruthless like blown chaff.

And it will happen in an instant,
suddenly!"

Isaiah [6][For they will][b] be visited by the LORD of Hosts,
with thunder and earthquake and a great sound,
whirlwind and tempest and a flame of a devouring fire.

[7]And the multitude of all the nations
that wage war against Ariel,
that attack it and its fortress and those who distress it,

will be like a dream,
a vision in the night—

[8][Yea][c], it will be [unto them even] as a hungry
person who dreams, and behold, he is eating
but awakens and his soul is empty;

or like a thirsty person who dreams,
and behold, he is drinking,
but awakens and behold, faint! And his soul is parched!

Thus, will be the multitude of all the nations
that wage war against Mount Zion.

[9][For behold, all you that do iniquity][d],
tarry and be astonished,
[for you will] blind yourselves and be blind;

[yea, you will be] drunk but not from wine;
[you will] stagger but not from strong drink.

[10]For [behold][e], the LORD has poured over
you a spirit of deep sleep.

---

the best sense in this passage. Hoskisson writes concerning the word in question, "that destroyed Judah will speak from the dead, that is, from the records they left behind, the Old Testament, and without the aid of a medium. This has nothing to do with necromancy and divination." Paul Hoskisson, "Update: The 'Familiar Spirit' in 2 Nephi 26:16," *Insights* 28, no. 6 (2008), 7.

a. Bracketed word is from JST.
b. Bracketed words are from JST.
c. Bracketed words in verse 8 are from JST and 2 Nephi 27:3.
d. All bracketed words in this verse are from JST and 2 Nephi 27:4.
e. All bracketed words in this verse are from JST and 2 Nephi 27:10.

[For behold, you have] shut your eyes,
[and you have rejected] the prophets and your rulers,
[and] the seers He has covered [because of your iniquities].

The Book of Mormon (29:11–14; JST 29:11–26)[a]

Isaiah [And it shall come to pass that the Lord God shall bring forth unto you the words of a book; and they shall be the words of them which have slumbered. (JST 29:11) And behold, the book shall be sealed; and in the book shall be a revelation from God, from the beginning of the world to the ending thereof. (JST 29:12) Wherefore, because of the things which are sealed up, the things which are sealed shall not be delivered in the day of the wickedness and abominations of the people. Wherefore, the book shall be kept from them. (JST 29:13) But the book shall be delivered unto a man, and he shall deliver the words of the book, which are the words of those who have slumbered in the dust; and he shall deliver these words unto another, but the words that are sealed he shall not deliver; neither shall he deliver the book. (JST 29:14)

For the book shall be sealed by the power of God, and the revelation which was sealed shall be kept in the book until the own due time of the Lord, that they may come forth; for behold, they reveal all things from the foundation of the world unto the end thereof. (JST 29:15) And the day cometh that the words of the book which were sealed shall be read upon the housetops; and they shall be read by the power of Christ; and all things shall be revealed unto the children of men, which ever have been among the children of men and which ever will be, even unto the end of the earth. (JST 29:16) Wherefore, at that day when the book shall be delivered unto the man of whom I have spoken, the book shall be hid from the eyes of the world, that the eyes of none shall behold it, save it be that three witnesses shall behold it by the power of God, besides him to whom the book shall be delivered; and they shall testify to the truth of the book and the things therein. (JST 29:17) And there is none other which shall view it, save it be a few according to the will of God, to bear testimony of his word unto the children of men; for the Lord God hath said that the words of the faithful should

a. Scholars have various views concerning the meaning of this section of Isaiah, but the Joseph Smith Translation (marked in brackets), provides us with great clarity and understanding.

speak, as it were, from the dead. (JST 29:18) Wherefore, the Lord God will proceed to bring forth the words of the book; and in the mouth of as many witnesses as seemeth him good will he establish his word; and woe be unto him that rejecteth the word of God. (JST 29:19) But behold, it shall come to pass that the Lord God shall say unto him to whom he shall deliver the book,

The Lord "Take these] words [which are not] sealed [and] deliver [them] to another, that he may show them unto the] learned, saying,

M. Harris 'Read this, I pray thee.' (JST 29:20 = KJV 29:11)

Isaiah And [the learned shall say,

C. Anthon "Bring hither the book, and I will read them";

The Lord and now because of the glory of the world and
to get gain will they say this, and not for the
glory of God. And the man shall say,

M. Harris "I cannot bring the book for it is sealed."

The Lord Then shall the learned say,]

C. Anthon "I cannot [read] it." (JST 29:21 = KJV 29:11)

Isaiah [Wherefore, it shall come to pass that the Lord God will deliver again] the book [and the words thereof] to him that is not learned; [and the man that is not learned shall say,

J. Smith "I am not learned."

Isaiah Then shall the Lord God say unto him,

The Lord "The learned shall not read them, for they have rejected them; and I am able to do mine own work; wherefore, thou shalt read the words which I shall give unto thee. (JST 29:22 = KJV 29:12) Touch not the things which are sealed, for I will bring them forth in mine own due time; for I will show unto the children of men that I am able to do mine own work. (JST 29:23) Wherefore, when thou hast read the words which I have commanded thee and obtained the witnesses which I have promised unto thee, then shalt thou seal up the book again and hide it up unto me, that I may preserve the words which thou hast not read until I shall see fit in mine own wisdom to reveal all things unto the children of men. (JST 29:24) For behold, I am God; and I am a God of miracles; and I will show unto the world that I am the same yesterday, today, and forever; and I work not among the children of men, save it be according to their faith."] (29:25)

Isaiah [And again, it shall come to pass that] the Lord [shall say unto him that shall read the words that shall be delivered to him]:

The Lord "Forasmuch as this people draw near
unto Me with their mouth,
and with their lips they honor Me,

but their [hearts] are far from Me,
and their fear [toward] Me is taught by the [precepts] of men.

Therefore, behold, I will proceed to do a marvelous work among this people, [yea], a marvelous work and a wonder, for the wisdom of their wise [and learned] shall perish, and the understanding of their prudent will be hid." (JST 29:26 = KJV 29:13–14)

The Humble Rejoice in the Book (29:15–24)

Isaiah 15 [And][a] woe to those who go deep to hide
their counsel from the Lord,
whose deeds are in the dark, and they say,

The wicked "Who sees us? And who knows us?"

Isaiah [And they also say]:

The wicked 16 "You turn things upside down! Should the
potter be regarded as the clay?"

The Lord ["But behold, I will show unto them," says the
Lord of Hosts, "that I know all their works].

The Lord Should the thing he made say of its maker,

Thing formed 'He did not make me'?

The Lord Or the thing formed say to the potter,

Thing formed 'He has no understanding'"?

Isaiah 17 [But behold, says the Lord of Hosts:

The Lord "I will show unto the children of men that it is][b] not yet a little while and Lebanon will be turned into a fertile field and the fertile field be regarded as a forest."

Isaiah 18 And in that day the deaf will hear the words of the book,
and from gloom and darkness the eyes of the blind will see.

---

a. Bracketed words in this verse are from 2 Nephi 27:27.

b. Words in the brackets are from 2 Nephi 27:28.

[19]And the meek also will increase {their}
rejoicing in the Lord;
and the poor will be joyful in the Holy One of Israel.

[20]For [assuredly as the Lord lives they shall see that][a]
the ruthless will come to nothing
and the scoffer cease.

And all who watch for iniquity will be cut off.
[21][And they][b], who, with a word, cause a person to sin
and who lay a snare for him who reproves in the gate
and turn aside the righteous for chaos.

[22]Therefore thus the Lord, who redeemed Abraham,
says to the house of Jacob:

The Lord "Jacob will not now be ashamed,
neither will his face now grow pale.

[23]Because when he sees his children, the work of
My hands, they will sanctify My name."

Isaiah And they will sanctify the Holy One of Jacob
and will hold in awe the God of Israel.

[24]They who err in spirit will know discernment;
those who murmur will learn instruction.

Judah Rejects Its Prophets and Walks with Egypt (30:1–17)

Isaiah **30** [1]Declares the Lord,

The Lord "Woe, stubborn children, who devise
counsel that is not from Me
and who form an alliance that is not of My
Spirit so that they add sin to sin,

[2]who go down to Egypt without asking at My mouth

to take refuge in the stronghold of Pharaoh
and to seek shelter in the shadow of Egypt.

[3]Therefore the stronghold of Pharaoh will be your shame
and the refuge in the shadow of Egypt your insult.

[4]Although his officials are in Zoan
and his envoys have reached Hanes,

a. Bracketed words are from 2 Nephi 27:31.
b. Bracketed words are from 2 Nephi 27:32.

5everyone will be put to shame, on account
of a people not able to profit them,
neither helping nor profiting, but shame, and disgrace, too."

6A prophecy against the Beasts of the Negev:
In the land of trouble and anguish,

lioness and lion among them,
viper and flying serpent.

They carry their riches on the backs of donkeys,
their treasures on the humps of camels, to a
people that cannot profit them.

7And Egypt is worthless!
They will help in vain!

Therefore, I have called her: "Its Arrogance Has Ceased!"

Isaiah 8Now come, write it on a tablet with them
and inscribe it on a book

and let it be for the last day,
a witness forever.

9For they are a rebellious people,
lying children—
children who are unwilling to hear the law of the Lord,

10who say to the seers,

The wicked "Do not see,"

Isaiah and to the prophets,

The wicked "Do not see right things.

Speak smooth things to us;
prophesy deceptions.

11Turn aside from the way;
turn off the path;
cause the Holy One of Israel to cease before us."

Isaiah 12Therefore, thus says the Holy One of Israel,

The Lord "Because you despise this word and trust in oppression
and perverseness and leaned on it,

13therefore, this iniquity will become to you like a breach,
bulging out in a high wall,

whose breaking comes suddenly,
in an instant.

[14]And its breaking is like a potter's vessel that
is broken, relentlessly shattered,
so that a shard will not be found among its fragments

with which to take fire from the hearth
or to dip up water out of a cistern."

Isaiah [15]For thus the Lord,
the LORD,
the Holy One of Israel said:

The LORD "In returning and rest you will be saved;
in quietness and in trust your strength will be.

But you were unwilling.
But you said,

Inhabitants of Judah [16]'No! Because upon a horse we will flee';

The LORD therefore, you will flee.

Inhabitants of Judah 'We will ride upon a swift one';

The LORD Therefore, your pursuers will be swift.

[17]One thousand before the threat of one;
before the threat of five, will you flee,

until you are left like a flagstaff on the top of a mountain,
like an ensign on a hill."

God's Grace and Compassion for Zion (30:18–26)

Isaiah [18]And therefore, the LORD waits to grant you grace,
and therefore, He will rise to show you compassion,

for the LORD is a God of justice;
blessed are all who wait for Him.

[19]Because, O people in Zion,
who dwell at Jerusalem,

surely you will weep no longer;
He will surely grant you grace at the sound of your crying;

when He hears it,
He will answer you.

[20]And the Lord will give you the bread of adversity
and the water of oppression,

and your Teacher will no longer hide Himself,
and your eyes will see your Teacher,

[21]and your ears will hear a word behind you, saying:

The Lord "This is the way;
walk in it,

whether you turn to the right
or you turn to the left."

Isaiah [22]Then you will defile your idols, overlaid with silver,
and your gold-plated molten images;

you will cast them away as menstrual cloth;
you will say to them,

God's covenant people "Go out!"

Isaiah [23]And He will give rain for your seed,
that you sow in the ground,
and bread, the produce of the ground,
which will be rich and fat.

In that day, your cattle will graze in a large pasture,
[24]and the oxen and the donkeys that work the
ground will eat seasoned fodder

that is winnowed with shovel and fork.

[25]And there will be on every lofty mountain
and every high hill, brooks running with water,

in the day of the great slaughter,
when towers fall.

[26]And the light of the moon will be as the light of the sun,
and the light of the sun will be sevenfold,
like the light of seven days,

in the day when the Lord binds up the
brokenness of His people
and heals the blow of their wound.

Joy for the Righteous During God's Judgments (30:27–33)

Isaiah [27]Behold, the name of the Lord comes from a distance,
His anger burning and the burden heavy,

His lips full of indignation,
and His tongue like a devouring fire;

[28]His breath is like an overflowing stream,
reaching up to the neck

to sift the nations with the sieve of destruction,
and a bridle on the jaws of the peoples, for he that leads astray.

[29]Your song will be as on the night when
a festival is sanctified,
and rejoicing of the heart, as when one walks with a flute

to come to the mountain of the LORD,
to the Rock of Israel.

[30]And the LORD will cause His majestic voice to be heard,
and He will show His arm coming down

with the indignation of anger
and a flame of devouring fire,

with a cloudburst
and tempest and hailstones.

[31]For at the voice of the LORD the Assyrians are terrified
when He smites with His rod.

[32]And every stroke with the appointed staff that the LORD
lays upon them is to the sound of tambourines and harps,
and in the wars that He will fight against them
is with brandished weapons.

[33]For a burning place was arranged long ago;
yea, it was prepared for the king.

Its pyre was made deep and wide,
with much fire and wood.

The breath of the LORD, like a stream of brimstone,
sets fire to it.

DIVINE PROTECTION FOR ZION AND JERUSALEM (31:1–9)

Isaiah

31 [1]Woe to those who go down to Egypt for help;
they rely on horses,

and they trust in chariots because they are many,
and in horsemen because they are very strong,

but do not look to the Holy One of Israel,
nor do they seek the LORD,

[2]and yet He is wise and brings disaster,
and He will not take back His words,

but He will rise against the house of evildoers
and against those who help workers of iniquity.

[3]The Egyptians are human and not God,
and their horses are flesh and not spirit.

When the Lord stretches out His hand,
the helper will stumble;
and he who is helped will fall,
and together they all will perish.

[4]For thus the Lord says to me,

The Lord "Just as the lion
or the young lion growls over his prey,

and though a group of shepherds is called forth against it,

it is not terrified by their voice,
nor is it disturbed at their noise."

Isaiah So, the Lord of Hosts will come down to fight for Mount Zion
and for its hill.

[5]Like birds hovering,
the Lord of Hosts will defend Jerusalem.

He will protect and deliver;
He will pass over and rescue.

Isaiah [6]Return to Him,
against whom the children of Israel have deeply revolted.

The Lord [7]"For in that day everyone will despise his idols of silver
and his idols of gold, which your sinful
hands have made for you.

[8]And the Assyrian will fall by a sword that is not of man,
and a sword, not of a human,

will devour him,
and he will flee from a sword,

and his young men will become forced laborers,
[9]and due to terror, he will pass to his stronghold,
and his officers will be terrified at the ensign,"

Isaiah declares the Lord, whose light is in Zion
and whose furnace is in Jerusalem.

King Messiah Reigns in Righteousness (32:1–8)

Isaiah

32 [1]Behold, a king will reign in righteousness,
and princes will govern in justice.

[2]And each will be like a refuge from the wind
and a shelter from the tempest,

like streams of water in a dry place,
like the shade of a great cliff in a weary land.

[3]And the eyes of those who see will not be closed,
and the ears of those who hear will listen,

[4]and the heart of the rash will understand knowledge,
and the tongue of the stammerers will speak fluently.

[5]The fool will no longer be called noble,
nor a villain said to be honorable.

[6]For the fool speaks folly,
and his heart works iniquity

to do ungodliness
and to speak error against the Lord,

to make empty the soul of the hungry
and to deprive the thirsty of drink.

[7]And the instruments of the villain are evil;
he devises wickednesses

to destroy the poor with lying words
when the needy speak justly.

[8]But the noble person makes noble plans,
and such rises to noble things.

Destruction for the Wicked, Peace for the Righteous (32:9–20)

The Lord

[9]"Women who are at ease, rise up, hear My voice!
And carefree daughters, give ear to My speech!

[10]Days beyond a year, carefree ones will quake,

because the vintage will fail,
the harvest will not come.

[11]Tremble, you women who are at ease;
quake, carefree ones;

strip
and make yourselves bare,

and gird {sackcloth} upon your waists,
12 beat on your breasts,

over pleasant fields,
over a fruitful vine;

13 On My people's soil
thorn and briar will come up,

yea, upon all the exulting houses, the town of revelry,

14 because the palaces will be forsaken,
the multitude of the [houses][a] shall be [desolate].

The citadel and watchtower will become
desolate spaces forever,

a joy of wild asses,
a pasture of flocks."

Isaiah 15 Until the Spirit from on high is poured out upon us,

and the wilderness becomes a fruitful field,
and the fruitful field is considered a forest.

16 Then justice will reside in the wilderness,
and righteousness will dwell in the fruitful field.

17 And the effect of righteousness will be peace,
and the work of righteousness, quietness and security forever.

The Lord 18 "And My people will live in a peaceful habitation,
in secure dwellings,
and in quiet resting places.

19 And when it hails, coming down on the forest,
and the city is totally laid low:[b]

20 Happy, you who sow beside all waters
and who let the ox and the donkey range free."

A Woe against Sennacherib? (33:1)

Isaiah 33 1 Woe, O destroyer, but you have not been destroyed,
and traitor, with whom none has betrayed.

When you stop destroying,
you will be destroyed;

a. Bracketed words in the verse are from JST.

b. The verse presents difficult forms, which makes a proper translation complicated.

when you make an end of betraying,
you will be betrayed.

THE RIGHTEOUS PRAISE THE LORD IN PRAYER (33:2–6)

God's covenant people

2"O LORD, be gracious to us;
we have waited[a] for You.

Be their arm every morning,
[their][b] salvation in time of trouble.

3At the tumultuous noise, peoples flee,
when You arise, nations scatter."

Isaiah

4And your spoil {O nations} is gathered
as the caterpillar gathers;
one leaps upon it as the locusts leap.

God's covenant people

5"The LORD is exalted,
for He dwells on high;

He fills Zion with justice and righteousness.
6And He will be faithfulness in your times,

a treasure of salvation, wisdom, and knowledge.
The fear of the LORD, that is his treasure."

THE WICKED ARE BURNED (33:7–14A)

Isaiah

7Behold the heroes cry outside;
the messengers of peace weep bitterly.

8Highways lie desolate,
the traveler ceases,

covenants are broken,
witnesses[c] are despised, there is respect for no one.

9The land mourns, grows weak;
Lebanon is ashamed, withers away.

Sharon is like a desert;
Bashan and Carmel are stripped bare.

The LORD

10"Now, I will arise,"

---

a. The Hebrew verb *qwh* ("waited") can also be rendered "hoped."

b. Bracketed word is from JST.

c. DSS Isaiah reads "witnesses" (Hebrew, *'adim*) versus MT's reading of "cities" (Hebrew, *'arim*), a case of graphically similar words.

Isaiah says the LORD.

The LORD "Now I will be exalted,
now I will lift Myself.

11 You conceive chaff,
you give birth to stubble;

your breath, as a fire, will consume you.
12 And peoples will be burnings of lime;
like thorns cut down, they will be burned in the fire.

13 Hear what I have done, you who are far off,
and know My might, you who are near."

14 The sinners in Zion are afraid;
trembling seizes the godless."

THE RIGHTEOUS WILL DWELL IN EVERLASTING BURNINGS (GLORY) WITH GOD (33:14B–17)

Isaiah 14 Who among us will dwell with devouring fire?
Who among us will dwell with everlasting burnings?

15 He who walks righteously
and speaks what is right,

he who rejects gain by extortion,
who shakes his hands from holding a bribe,

who stops his ears from hearing of bloodshed
and shuts his eyes from seeing evil.

16 He will dwell on the heights;
his place of defense will be fortresses of rocks.

His bread will be given;
his water will be sure.

17 Your eyes will see the King in His beauty;
they will see a land that is far off.

THE GLORIOUS CONDITIONS OF ZION (33:18–24)

Isaiah 18 Your heart will meditate on the terror:

Unnamed individual "Where is the one who counts {the taxes}?
Where is he who weighs {the tribute}?
Where is he who counts the towers?"

Isaiah

[19]You will not see a fierce people,
people of unintelligible speech,

which you cannot comprehend,
a strange tongue, which you cannot understand.

[20]Behold Zion,
the town of our appointed festivals;

your eyes will see Jerusalem, a peaceful habitation,
a tent not moved,

its stakes not pulled up forever,
and its cords never broken.

[21]For there the Lord in majesty will be for us,
a place of rivers, wide streams;

no oared ship will travel it,
nor mighty ship will pass on it.

[22]For the Lord is our judge,
the Lord is our lawgiver,

the Lord is our king;
He will save us.

[23]Your ropes have come loose;
they cannot hold the base of their mast,
nor keep the sail spread out.

Then the abundant spoil was divided;
the lame have taken the plunder.

[24]And no resident will say,

Unnamed individual

"I am sick."

Isaiah

The people who dwell there are forgiven of iniquity.

A Day of Wrath upon Edom (the World) (34:1–8)

Isaiah

34 [1]Come near, O nations, to hear,
and hearken, O peoples!

Let the earth and its fulness hear,
the world, and all that comes from it.

[2]For the Lord has wrath against all nations
and anger against all their host.

He has destroyed them,
given them to the slaughter.

3 Their slain will be cast out,
and the stench of their corpses will rise;

mountains will flow from their blood,
the valleys[a] will be split.

4 All the host of heaven will be dissolved,
and the heavens will roll up like a scroll,

and all their host will wither, as the leaf withers on a vine,
and like withered fruit on a fig tree.

The Lord 5 "For My sword is bathed in heaven;
behold, it descends upon Edom

and upon the people promised for destruction,
for judgment."

Isaiah 6 The Lord's sword is filled with blood;
it is gorged with fat

from the blood of lambs and goats,
from the fat of the kidneys of rams,

because the Lord has a sacrifice in Bozrah
and a great slaughter in the land of Edom.

7 And wild oxen will go down with them,
and the bulls with the mighty ones,

and their land will be drunken with blood,
and their soil will be made rich with fat.

8 For it is a day of the Lord's vengeance,
a year of recompenses for the cause of Zion.

Edom (the World) to Be Burned (34:9–15)

Isaiah 9 And the streams {of Edom} will be turned to pitch,
and its soil to brimstone,
and its land will become burning pitch.

10 Night and day it will not be extinguished;
forever its smoke will rise.

---

a. The reading of "valleys," which completes the parallelism, comes from the DSS Isaiah scrolls.

From generation to generation, it will lie waste;
none will pass through for ever and ever.

11 Hawk and hedgehog will possess it,
and owl and raven will dwell in it.

And He will stretch a line of chaos over it,
and a measuring line of desolation.

12 Its nobles—there is no one there to call it a kingdom,
and all its princes will be nothing.

13 And thorns will come up in its palaces,
nettles and thistles in its fortresses.

It will be the habitation of jackals,
an enclosure for ostriches.

14 And wild beasts will meet with hyenas,
and wild goats will call to each other;

yea, a night creature will settle
and find itself a resting place.

15 An owl will nest there and lay eggs
and hatch them and gather her young in her shadow.

Yea, vultures will be gathered there,
each one with its female companion.

The Book of the Lord (34:16–17)

The Lord (to His people)

16 "Examine the book of the Lord,
and read [the names written therein][a].

Not one will be missing;
none will lack [their] female companion,

for My mouth has commanded,
and [My] Spirit has gathered them.

17 And [I] have cast a lot for them,
and [I have] divided it to them by measuring line.

They will possess it forever;
from generation to generation, they will dwell in it."

a. The words enclosed in brackets in verses 16–17 are from the JST.

Latter-day Israel Rejoices and Blossoms as a Rose (35:1–10)

Isaiah

35 1 The wilderness and dry land will exult,
and let the desert be joyful and blossom like the rose.

2 It surely will blossom and be joyful,
yea, joy and singing gladly,

the glory of Lebanon is given to it,
the majesty of Carmel and Sharon,

and they will see the glory of the Lord
and the majesty of our God.

3 Strengthen the weak hands,
and make firm the feeble knees.

4 Say to those who have an anxious heart:

Unnamed individuals

"Be strong, do not fear!

Behold, your God will come with vengeance;
God will come with divine retribution and save you."

Isaiah

5 Then the eyes of the blind will be opened
and the ears of the deaf opened.

6 Then the lame will leap like deer,
and the tongue of the mute will sing gladly.

For waters will break forth in the wilderness,
and streams in the desert,

7 and the parched ground will become a pool,
and the thirsty ground, springs of water.

The habitation of jackals will become a grassy place of rest,
with reeds and rushes.

8 And a highway will be there,
[for][a] a way [will be cast up].

It will be called:

Unnamed individuals

"The Way of Holiness."

Isaiah

The unclean will not pass over [upon] it,
but it will be [cast up] for those [who are clean,

and] the wayfaring men,
though [they are accounted] fools, will not err there.

---

a. Bracketed words in verses 8–10 are from JST.

[9]No lion will be there,
nor violent beasts will go up on it;
they will not be found there!

And the redeemed will go,
[10]and the ransomed of the LORD will return

and will come to Zion with songs
and everlasting joy upon their heads;

they will obtain exultation and rejoicing,
and sorrow and sighing will flee.

SENNACHERIB, KING OF ASSYRIA, THREATENS JERUSALEM (36:1–22)

Isaiah

36 [1]And it came to pass in the fourteenth year of King Hezekiah, Sennacherib king of Assyria came up against all
the fortified cities of Judah and seized them. [2]And the king of
Assyria sent the chief officer from Lachish to Jerusalem with a
great army to King Hezekiah. And he stood by the aqueduct of
the Upper Pool on the road to the Washer's Field. [3]And Eliakim,
the son of Hilkiah, who was over the house; Shebna, the scribe;
and Joah, the son of Asaph, the recorder, went out to him. [4]And
the chief officer said to them:

Chief officer

"Say to Hezekiah, please—Thus says the great king, the king of
Assyria, 'What is this trust in which you have trusted? [5]I say,
'[Your] words [are but vain, when you say][a], 'I have counsel and
strength for war.' Now, on whom do you trust, that you have
rebelled against me?

[6]Behold, you are trusting on Egypt, that broken reed of a staff,
which pierces the palm of anyone who leans on it; such is Pharaoh, the king of Egypt, to all who trust him.

[7]But if you say to me, 'We trust in the LORD, our God'—Did not
Hezekiah remove his high places and altars, saying to Judah
and Jerusalem, 'You will worship before this altar?'

[8]And now, please, make a pledge with my master, the king
of Assyria. Let me give you two thousand horses, if you can
set riders upon them. [9]How then can you turn aside a single
captain of the least of my master's servants, when you trust in

---

a. Bracketed words in verse 5 are from JST.

Egypt for chariots and for horsemen? 10 And now, is it without the Lord that I have come up against this land to destroy it? The Lord said to me, 'Go up against this land and destroy it.'"

Isaiah 11 Then Eliakim, and Shebna, and Joah said to the chief officer,

Eliakim, Shebna, and Joah "Speak, please, to your servants in Aramaic, for we understand it. Do not speak to us in the language of Judah within the hearing of the people who are on the wall."

Isaiah 12 But the chief officer said,

Chief officer "Did my master send me to speak these words to you and your master, and not to the men sitting on the wall? They are doomed, with you, to eat their own dung and to drink their own urine."

Isaiah 13 Then the chief officer stood and called out with a loud voice and in the language of Judah, and he said,

Chief officer "Hear the words of the great king, the king of Assyria. 14 Thus says the king: 'Do not let Hezekiah deceive you, for he will not be able to deliver you. 15 Do not allow Hezekiah to persuade you to trust in the Lord by saying, Surely, the Lord will save us. This city will not be given into the hand of the king of Assyria.' 16 Do not listen to Hezekiah, for thus says the king of Assyria, 'Make a blessing[a] with me and come out to me; then everyone will eat of his own vine and every one of his own fig tree, and every one of you will drink the water of his own cistern, 17 until I come and take you to a land like your land, a land of grain and wine, a land of bread and vineyards. 18 Lest Hezekiah mislead you, saying, 'The Lord will deliver us.' Did the gods of the nations ever deliver each its land from the hand of the king of Assyria? 19 Where are the gods of Hamath and Arpad? Where are the gods of Sepharvaim, and did they deliver Samaria from my hand? 20 Who among all the gods of these countries has delivered their countries from my hand, that the Lord will deliver Jerusalem out of my hand?"

Isaiah 21 But they were silent and did not answer him, for it was the command of the king, saying,

Hezekiah "Do not answer him."

---

a. This literal translation is a sham, designed to make the people think that paying a tribute is a blessing. But the king is really saying "pay me tribute."

Isaiah

22Then Eliakim, the son of Hilkiah, who was over the house; Shebna, the scribe; and Joah, the son of Asaph, the recorder, came to Hezekiah, with their garments rent, and they told him the words of the chief officer.

Hezekiah Seeks Isaiah's Counsel and Prays in the Temple (37:1–20)

Isaiah

37 1And it came to pass when King Hezekiah heard it, he tore his clothes and covered himself with sackcloth and went into the House of the Lord. 2And he sent Eliakim, who was over the house; Shebna, the scribe; and the elders of the priests, who had covered themselves with sackcloth, to Isaiah, the prophet, son of Amoz. 3And they said to him,

Eliakim and Shebna

"Thus says Hezekiah, 'This day is a day of distress, rebuke, and disgrace because children have come to the point of birth, but there is no strength to give birth. 4Perhaps the Lord your God hears the words of the chief officer, whom the king of Assyria his master has sent to taunt the living God, and the Lord your God will rebuke the words that He has heard. Therefore, may you lift up a prayer for the remnant who remain.'"

Isaiah

5And the ministers of King Hezekiah came to Isaiah. 6And Isaiah said to them,

Isaiah

"Thus, you will say to your master, Thus says the Lord,

The Lord

'Do not be afraid of the words that you have heard, with which the youths of the king of Assyria have blasphemed Me. 7Behold, I am putting a spirit in him so that he will hear a rumor and return to his land, and in his land, I will make him fall by the sword.'"

Isaiah

8The chief officer returned and found the king of Assyria fighting against Libnah, for he had heard that he had left Lachish. 9And he heard about Tirhakah, king of Cush saying, "He has gone forth to war with you." And he sent messengers to Hezekiah, saying,

Chief officer

10"Thus, you will say to Hezekiah, king of Judah, saying, 'Do not let your God, who you trust, deceive you by saying, Jerusalem will not be given into the hand of the king of Assyria. 11Behold, you have heard what the kings of Assyria have done to all the countries, completely destroying them, and you will be delivered? 12Have the gods delivered the nations that my fathers destroyed—Gozen, Haran, Rezeph, and the people of Eden who were in Telassar? [13]Where is the king of Hamath, and the king of Arpad, and the kings of the cities of Sepharvaim, Hena, and Ivvah?'"

Isaiah [14]And Hezekiah took the letter from the hand of the messengers and read it. Then he went up to the House of the LORD and spread it before the LORD. [15]And Hezekiah prayed to the LORD, saying,

Hezekiah [16]"O LORD of Hosts, the God of Israel, enthroned on the cherubim, You alone are God of all the kingdoms of the earth; You have made the heavens and the earth. [17]Extend Your ear, O LORD, and hear. Open Your eyes, O LORD, and see. And hear all the words of Sennacherib, which he has sent to taunt the living God. [18]Truly, O LORD, the kings of Assyria have destroyed all the nations and their lands [19]and have placed their gods into the fire; they have destroyed them because they were not gods, but the work of the hands of a human—wood and stone. [20]And now, O LORD our God, save us from his hand, that all the kingdoms of the earth may know that You alone are the LORD."

THE LORD RESPONDS—SENNACHERIB WILL FALL (37:21–38)

Isaiah [21]Then Isaiah, the son of Amoz, sent to Hezekiah saying, "Thus says the LORD, the God of Israel, 'of which you prayed to Me about Sennacherib, the king of Assyria,' [22]This is the word that the LORD has spoken concerning him:

The LORD "The virgin Daughter of Zion, she scorns you! She mocks you!
The Daughter of Jerusalem, she wags
her head behind your back.

[23]Whom have you taunted and blasphemed?
Against whom have you raised your voice
and lifted your eyes up high? Against the Holy One of Israel!

[24]You have taunted the Lord by the hand
of your servants. And you said,

Sennacherib 'With my many chariots I have gone up to the heights of the mountains, to the far parts of Lebanon. And I cut down its tall cedars and its choicest cypresses. I came to its remotest height, its most fruitful forest. [25]I dug wells and drank the water of foreigners[a]. I dried up all the streams of Egypt with the sole of my foot.'

---

a. This reading comes from DSS Isaiah and the parallel passage of 2 Kings 19:24.

The LORD 26 Have you not heard long ago
that which I have done from days of old?

I fashioned it;
I brought it to pass—

that you should make fortified cities desolate,
into heaps, to be destroyed.

27 And their inhabitants are short of power;
they are dismayed and confounded.

and have become grass of the field,
and the green herb,

grass on the rooftops
and a field before an east wind[a].

28 I know your standing up[b], and your sitting,
and your going out, and your coming in,
and your rage against Me.

29 Because of your raging against Me,
and your arrogance has come to My ears,
I will put My hook in your nose
and My bit in your lips,
and I will turn you back by the way that you came."

30 And this is the sign for you:
Eat what grows of itself this year,
and in the second year what springs of the same,
but in the third year, sow and reap
and plant vineyards and eat their fruit.

31 And the remnant of the house of Judah
will again take root below
and bear fruit above.

32 For out of Jerusalem will go forth a remnant,
and they that escape [from Jerusalem will
come upon][c] Mount Zion."

Isaiah The zeal of the LORD of Hosts will do this.

33 Therefore, thus says the LORD concerning
the king of Assyria,

---

a. Reading from DSS Isaiah.

b. From DSS Isaiah.

c. Bracketed words in this section are from the JST.

The Lord "He will not come into this city,
or shoot an arrow there,

or come before it with a shield,
or cast up a siege-ramp against it.

34 By the way that he came, he will return.
And he will not come into this city,"

Isaiah declares the Lord.

The Lord 35 "I will defend this city, to save it for My own sake
and for the sake of David, My servant."

Isaiah 36 And the angel of the Lord went forth and slew a hundred
and eighty-five thousand in the Assyrian camp. And when
they [who were left] arose early in the morning, behold, they
were all dead corpses. 37 And Sennacherib, the king of Assyria,
traveled and returned and dwelt at Nineveh. 38 And as he was
worshipping in the house [temple] of Nisroch, his god, his sons,
Adrammelech and Sharezer, slew him with the sword. And they
escaped into the land of Armenia. Then Esarhaddon, his son,
reigned in his stead.

King Hezekiah's Sickness (38:1–8)

Isaiah 38 1 In those days Hezekiah became sick to the point
of death. Isaiah, the prophet, the son of Amoz,
came to him and said to him, "Thus says the Lord,

The Lord 'Set your house in order, because you will
die; and you will not live.'"

Isaiah 2 Then Hezekiah turned his face to the wall and
prayed to the Lord. 3 And he said,

Hezekiah "Please, O Lord, remember now how I have walked
before you in truth and with a whole heart, and
I have done what is good in your sight."

Isaiah And Hezekiah wept bitterly. 4 And the word of
the Lord came to Isaiah, saying,

The Lord 5 "Go and say to Hezekiah, 'Thus says the Lord, the God of
David your father, I have heard your prayer. I have seen your
tears. Behold, I will add fifteen years to your days. 6 And I will
deliver you and this city out of the hand of the king of Assyria,
and I will defend this city.'"

Isaiah [21]Isaiah said, "Let them take a cake of figs and apply to
the boil that he may recover." Also, Hezekiah said,

Hezekiah [22]"What is the sign that I will go up to
the House of the Lord?"[a]

Isaiah [7]And this is the sign to you from the Lord that the Lord
will do this thing concerning which He has spoken:

The Lord [8]'Behold, I will turn back the shadow cast by the sun, which
had descended on the steps of Ahaz, by ten steps.'"

Isaiah Then the sun turned back the ten steps it had descended.

King Hezekiah's Psalm (38:9–20)

Isaiah [9]A writing of Hezekiah, king of Judah, after he had
been sick and had recovered from his sickness:

Hezekiah [10]I said in the half of my days, "I will go
into the gates of Sheol.[b]
I am deprived of the rest of my years."

[11]I said, "I will not see the LORD in the land of the living;
I will not look upon a human again, or
the inhabitants of the world.

[12]My dwelling is pulled up
and is removed from me like a tent of a shepherd.

I have rolled up my life like a weaver;
from the loom He has cut me away.

From day to night, You have finished me.
[13]I cried out until morning; like a lion He broke all my bones.
From day to night, You have finished me.

[14]I chirp, like a swallow, a crane;
I moan like a dove.

---

a Apparently Isaiah 38 21–22 have been misplaced, and they likely belong in the text here, between verses 6 and 7. This is (1) the reading of 2 Kings 20:6–9, a text that parallels this part of Isaiah; (2) the context of these passages; and (3) the evidence of the Isaiah Scroll. Verses 21–22 of that scroll were copied after verse 20, by a later scribe, making their placement there questionable.

b. On the meaning of the Hebrew word *sheol*, see Isaiah 5:14, footnote a.

My eyes grow weary from looking upward. O Lord, I am in distress; be my pledge of surety. 15 What can I say? Since He has responded to me, and He has [healed me].[a] All my years I move slowly [that I may not walk] in the bitterness of my soul.

16 O Lord, [You who are] the life of my spirit, [in whom I live],
may You restore me to health and cause me to live;

[and in all these things I will praise you]. 17 Behold, it was bitterness for me, bitterness [instead of peace]. But You in love have saved me from the pit of destruction, for You have cast all my sins behind Your back.

18 For Sheol[b] does not thank You,
death does not praise You,

those who go down to the pit do not hope for Your truth. 19 The living, the living, he will thank You, like me on this day. A father makes known Your truth to the children. 20 O Lord, save me, and we will play music on stringed instruments, all the days of our lives in the House of the Lord."

Isaiah's Prophecy of Babylonian Captivity (39:1–8)

Isaiah 39 1 At that time Merodach-baladan, son of Baladan, king of Babylon, sent letters and a gift to Hezekiah, when he had heard that he had been sick and had regained strength. 2 Hezekiah rejoiced concerning them, and he showed them the house of his treasure, the silver and the gold, and the spices, and the precious oil, and all his armory, and all that was found in his treasuries. There was nothing in his house, nor in all his dominion, that Hezekiah did not show them. 3 Then Isaiah, the prophet, came to King Hezekiah and said to him, "What did these men say to you? And from where did they come to you?" And Hezekiah said,

Hezekiah "They have come to me from a far country, from Babylon."

Isaiah 4 And he said, "What have they seen in your house?" And Hezekiah said,

Hezekiah "They have seen all that is in my house. There is not a thing that I did not show them in my treasuries."

a. Bracketed words in verses 14–16 are from JST.

b. On the meaning of the Hebrew word *sheol*, see Isaiah 5:14, footnote a.

Isaiah

5 Then Isaiah said to Hezekiah, "Hear the word of the LORD of
Hosts."

The LORD

6 "Behold, the days are coming when everything that is in your
house, and that your fathers have stored until this day will be
carried to Babylon; not a thing will be left, says the LORD. 7 And
some of your sons, who will come from you, who will be born to
you—they will be taken and will become eunuchs in the palace
of the king of Babylon."

Isaiah

8 And Hezekiah said to Isaiah,

Hezekiah

"The word of the LORD is good that you have spoken."

Isaiah

And he said,

Hezekiah

"Because there will be peace and truth in my days."

THE LORD'S MESSAGE OF COMFORT TO JERUSALEM (40:1–8)

The LORD

40 1 "Comfort, O comfort My people,"

Isaiah

says your God.

2 Speak to the heart of Jerusalem
and call to it,

because its hard service is fulfilled,
because its iniquity is pardoned,
because it has taken from the LORD's
hand, double for all its sins.

3 A voice of one calling in the wilderness,

John the Baptist

"Prepare the way of the LORD;
make straight in the desert a highway for our God."

Isaiah

4 Every valley will be lifted up,
and every mountain and hill will be made low;

the uneven ground will become level,
and the rough places a plain.

5 Then the glory of the LORD will be revealed,
and all flesh will see it together,
for the mouth of the LORD has spoken.

6 A voice said,

The LORD

"Call out!"

Isaiah

And I said, "What will I call out?"

The Lord "All flesh is grass,
and all its loving-kindness like the flower of the field."

Isaiah 7 Grass withers,
a flower fades
when the Lord's Spirit blows upon it.

Surely, the people are grass.
8 Grass withers;
a flower fades,
but the word of our God stands forever.

The Lord Comes Like a Shepherd (40:9–11)

Isaiah 9 O Zion, that brings good tidings, go up on a high mountain;
O Jerusalem, that brings good tidings,
lift your voice with power.

O lift up, fear not, say to the cities of Judah,

Zion's inhabitants "Behold your God!

10 Behold, the Lord, the Lord will come with strength,
and His arm rules for Him.

Behold, His reward is with Him,
and His recompense is before Him.

11 Like a shepherd He will tend His flock;
He will gather lambs in His arm,

and He will carry them in His bosom.
He will lead the sucklings."

Who Is Like unto the Lord? (40:12–25)

Isaiah 12 Who has measured the waters in the hollow of His hand,
and marked off the heavens with the width of His hand,
and gauged the dust of the earth in a measure?

And weighed the mountains in the scales
and the hills in a balance?

13 Who directs the Spirit of the Lord?
Or what man shows Him his counsel?

14 With whom did He counsel? Who made Him understand,
and who taught Him the path of justice,

and taught Him knowledge,
and made Him know the way of understanding?

[15]Behold, the nations are like a drop from a bucket,
and they are regarded as dust on the scales;
behold, He takes up the isles like fine dust.

[16]And Lebanon is not sufficient for burning,
and its beasts are not sufficient for a burnt offering.

[17]All nations are as nothing before Him.
They are regarded by Him as nothingness and chaos.

[18]Then, to whom will you liken God?
Or with what likeness do you compare Him?

[19]A craftsman casts the idol,
and a smith overlays it with gold and forges chains of silver.

[20]The poor chooses an offering of wood that will not rot.
He seeks for himself a skilled craftsman to
prepare an idol that will not topple.

[21]Will you not know?
Will you not hear?

Has it not been told to you from the beginning?
Have you not understood from the foundations of the earth?

[22]He who is enthroned above the circle of the earth
and its inhabitants are like grasshoppers,

who stretches out the heavens like a curtain
and stretches them like a tent to dwell in,

[23]who brings rulers to nothing.
He makes the judges of the earth as chaos.

[24]No sooner are they planted,
no sooner are they sown,
no sooner has their stem taken root in the earth,

when He blows upon them and they wither,
and the tempest carries them off like stubble.

The Lord [25]"To whom will you liken Me,
that I may be compared?"

Isaiah says the Holy One.

The Lord Sustains His People with His Power (40:26–31)

Isaiah [26]Lift up your eyes on high and see—
Who created these?

He who brings out their hosts by number,
calling them all by name.

Through abundant might and mighty power,
not one is missing.

27 Why do you say, O Jacob,
and speak, O Israel?

God's covenant people

"My way is hidden from the Lord,
and from my God my judgment is passed over?"

Isaiah

28 Did you not know?
Did you not hear?

The Lord is the Everlasting God,
Creator of the ends of the earth!

He does not faint;
He is not weary.

His understanding is unsearchable.

29 He gives power to the faint,
and to him who lacks might, He increases strength.

30 Even youth will grow faint and weary,
and young men will certainly stumble,

31 but those who wait for the Lord will renew their strength;
they will go up with wings like eagles,

they will run and not grow weary,
and they will walk and not faint.

Israel Is the Lord's Servant (41:1–20)

The Lord

41 1 "Be silent before Me, O islands,
and let the peoples renew their strength;

let them approach,
then let them speak:

People

'Let us draw near together for judgment.'"

Isaiah or the Lord

2 Who stirred up a righteous one from the east,
calling him to his feet?

He gives up nations before him
and made him rule over kings,

who makes them like dust with his sword,
like wind-scattered stubble with his bow.

3 He subjugates them, he passes in peace,
by paths his feet have not trod.

4 Who has performed and done this, calling the
generations from the beginning?

The Lord "I, the Lord am the first,
and with the last ones, I am He!

5 The islands have seen and feared;
the ends of the earth tremble.

They have drawn near,
and they have come.

Everyone 6 Everyone helps his neighbor
and to his brother says,

Craftsman 'Be strong.'

7 And the craftsman strengthens the smith;
the hammer wielder strengthens the anvil pounder.
He says to the soldering:

The Lord 'It {the idol} is good,'

And he strengthens it {the idol} with nails
so that it will not totter.

8 And you, Israel, are My servant,
Jacob, whom I have chosen,

the offspring of Abraham,
My friend,

9 whom I strengthened from the ends of the earth,
and from its farthest corners called to you, saying,

'I have chosen you,
and I have not rejected you.

10 Fear not, for I am with you;
do not be afraid, for I am your God.

I will strengthen you,
also, I will help you,

also, I will uphold you
with My right hand, My righteousness.'

11 Behold, all who are angry with you will
be ashamed and confounded;
those who strive against you will be as
nothing and will perish.

12 You will seek those who contend with you,
but you will not find them.

Those who war against you will be as nothing,
and as nothingness.

13 For I, the Lord, your God, grasp your right hand.
It is I who say to you:

'Do not fear, I am helping you.
14 Do not fear, O worm of Jacob, men of
Israel, I am helping you,"

Isaiah declares the Lord
and your Redeemer,
the Holy One of Israel.

The Lord 15 "Behold, I make of you a threshing instrument,
a new one, having two edges;

you will thresh and crush mountains,
and you will make the hills like chaff.

16 You will winnow them, and the wind will carry them away,
and the tempest will scatter them.

And you will be joyful in the Lord;
you will glory in the Holy One of Israel.

17 The poor and the needy seek water, but there is none.
Their tongue is parched with thirst.

I, the Lord, will answer them;
I, the God of Israel, will not forsake them.

18 I will open rivers on the barren heights
and fountains in the valleys.

I will make the wilderness a pool of water
and the parched land springs of water.

19 I will place in the wilderness the cedar,
acacia, myrtle, and olive tree;
I will set in the desert the cypress, plane,
and pine trees together."

Isaiah [20]So that they may see and know,
and they may consider and understand together

that the hand of the Lord has done this,
and the Holy One of Israel has created it.

Graven Images Are Chaos, Nothing, and Emptiness (41:21–29)

The Lord [21]"Set forth your case,"

Isaiah says the Lord.

The Lord "Bring forth your evidences,"

Isaiah says the King of Jacob.

The Lord [22]"Let them [graven images] bring forth
and tell us what will happen.
Tell us the former things, what they are, that
our heart may consider them,

and then we may know their outcome,
or declare to us the things that are to come.

[23]Tell us what is to come hereafter, that we
may know that you are gods;
yea, do good or do evil, that we may be
frightened and see together.

[24]Behold, you are nothing,
and your work is worthless!

He who chooses you is an abomination.

[25]I stirred up one from the north, and he has come,
and from the rising of the sun, he will call on My name,

and he will come on rulers as on mortar
and as the potter tramples clay.

[26]Who declared it from the beginning, that we might know?
Or beforehand, that we might say, 'He is righteous?'

Yea, there are none who declare,
yea, there are none who announce,
yea, there are none who hear your sayings.

[27]First for Zion, behold, here they are,
and I will give to Jerusalem one who brings good tidings.

[28]And I looked, and there is no one;
and among them [the false gods], there is no counselor,
whom I asked, that could answer a word.

[29]Behold, they are all chaos,
their works are nothing,
their molten images are wind and emptiness."

A Prophecy of Jesus Christ's Mission and Ministry (42:1–9)

The Lord

42 [1]"Behold, My servant, whom I uphold,
My chosen, in whom my soul delights.

I have put My spirit upon him;
he will bring justice to the nations.

[2]He will not cry out or lift his voice,
nor make it heard outside.

[3]He will not break a crushed reed,
and He will not quench a faltering wick;
He will bring forth justice in truth.

[4]He will not falter
nor be discouraged

until He has established justice in the earth,
and the islands will wait for His law."

Isaiah

[5]Thus says God, the Lord,

Creator of the heavens, and He stretches them out,
He spreads forth the earth and that which comes from it,

He gives breath to the people upon it
and spirit to those who walk on it.

The Lord

[6]"I, the Lord, have called you in righteousness;
I grasp your hand and I keep you,

and I give you for a covenant of the people,
for a light to the nations,
[7]to open blind eyes,

to bring out the prisoner from prison
and those who sit in darkness from the dungeon.

[8]I am the Lord,
that is My name,

and I will not give My glory to another,
neither My praise to graven images.

[9] Behold, the former things have come to pass,
and I declare new things:
I tell you of them before they spring forth."

A Hymn to Jehovah, the Redeemer (42:10–17)

Isaiah

[10] Sing a new song to the Lord,
His praise from the end of the earth,

you who go down to the sea and all that is in it,
the islands and their dwellers.

[11] Let the wilderness and its cities lift their voices,
the villages that Kedar inhabits;

let the inhabitants of Sela sing gladly,
let them shout from the top of the mountains.

[12] Let them give glory to the Lord
and declare His praise in the islands.

[13] The Lord goes forth like a warrior;
He stirs up fury, like a man of war.

He cries out, yea, He roars;
He prevails over His enemies.

The Lord

[14] "I have kept silent a long time;
I keep still,
I restrain myself;

like a woman in labor, I will cry out;
I will gasp,
and I will pant at the same time.

[15] I will lay waste mountains and hills,
and I will dry up all their vegetation;

and I will turn rivers into islands,
and I will dry up pools.

[16] And I will lead the blind in a way that they have not known;
I will guide them in paths that they have not known;

I will turn darkness into light before them
and rough places into level ground.

These are the things I will do,
and I will not forsake them.

17 They have turned backward;
they are certainly ashamed,

who trust in an idol,
who say to molten images,

Idolaters 'You are our gods.'"

The Servant to the Blind (42:18–25)

The Lord 18 "O deaf ones, hear!
And O blind ones, look, that you may see!

19 [For I will send My servant unto you][a] who [are] blind, [yea,
a messenger to open the eyes of the blind and unstop the ears
of the] deaf; [and they shall be made] perfect [notwithstanding
their blindness, if they will hearken unto the messenger], the
Lord's servant."

Isaiah 20 [You are a people] who have seen many things, but you do
not observe,

opening the ears [to hear],
but [you] will not hear.

21 The Lord is [not] pleased [with such a people, but] for His
righteousness' sake, He will magnify the law and make it glorious.

22 [You are] a plundered and looted people;
[your enemies], all of them, [have] snared [you] in holes,

and [they have hid you] in prison houses.
[They have taken you]

for a plunder, but none delivers,
for a spoil, and none says, "Restore."

23 Who among [them][b] gives ear to [you],
[or] will hearken and hear [you], for the time to come?

24 [And] who gave Jacob for a spoil
and Israel to the plunderers?

---

a. Bracketed words in verses 19–25 are from JST.

b. Bracketed words in verses 19–25 are from JST.

Did not the Lord,
He against whom they have sinned?

For they were not willing to walk in His ways
and did not heed His law;

25 therefore, He has poured fury upon them,
His anger, and the strength of battle;

and [they have] set [them] on fire round
about, yet [they know] not;
and it burned [them], yet [they] laid it not to heart.

Prophecy of the Savior and Redemption (43:1–7)

Isaiah

43 1 And now, thus says the Lord, your Creator, O Jacob,
And your Fashioner, O Israel:

The Lord

"Fear not, for I have redeemed you;
I have called you by name, you are Mine.

2 When you pass through the waters, I am with you;
and through the rivers, they will not overwhelm you.

When you walk through fire, you will not be scorched,
and the flames will not burn you.

3 For I am the Lord, your God,
the Holy One of Israel, your Savior!

I give Egypt for your ransom[a],
Cush and Seba in exchange for you.

4 Because you are precious in My eyes,
you are honored, and I love you;

I give a human in return for you,
people in exchange for your life.

5 Fear not,
for I am with you.

I will bring your offspring from the east,
and I will gather you from the west.

---

a. "Ransom" (Hebrew, *kofer*) can also be translated "redemption payment." The Lord pays a ransom or redemption payment to free Israel (from the nations, just as He freed ancient Israel from the dominance of Egypt), but instead of money, He exchanges three countries—Egypt, Cush, and Seba—for Israel.

[6]I will say to the north, 'Give up,'
and to the south, "Do not withhold!

Bring my sons from afar
and my daughters from the end of the earth.

[7]All who are called by My name,
and for My glory I created them—

I fashioned them,
I created them."

We Are Witnesses That the Lord Is God (43:8–13)

Isaiah [8]Bring forth a blind people who have eyes,
and those who are deaf who have ears.

[9]Let all nations gather together,
and let the peoples assemble.

Who among them will declare this
and make us hear the former things?

Let them bring their witnesses to prove them right,
and let them hear and say,

Witnesses "It is truth."

The Lord [10]"You are My witnesses,"

Isaiah declares the Lord,

The Lord "and My servant whom I have chosen,

so that you may know and trust in Me
and understand that I am He;

there was no god formed before Me,
nor will there be after Me.

[11]I, I am the Lord,
and there is no Savior besides Me.

[12]I have declared,
and I have saved,

and I have proclaimed—and there is no
strange god among you—
and you are My witnesses, that I am God,"

Isaiah declares the Lord.

The Lord [13]"Yea, before the day was, I am He; there is none that can
deliver from My hand; I act, and who will reverse it?"

THE LORD PROVIDES WATER FOR US (43:14–21)

Isaiah

14 Thus says the LORD,
your Redeemer,
the Holy One of Israel,

The LORD

"For your sake I send to Babylon,
and I bring down all of them as fugitives,
and the shouting of the Chaldeans will become lamentations.

15 I am the LORD, your Holy One,
the Creator of Israel, your King."

Isaiah

16 Thus says the LORD, who makes a way in the sea
and a path in the mighty waters,

17 who brings forth chariot and horse,
together with army and warrior.

They lie down; they cannot rise.
They are out, snuffed like a wick.

The LORD

18 "Do not remember the former things
nor consider the things of old.

19 Behold, I am doing a new thing;
now, it will spring forth. Do you not know it?

Also, I will make a way in the wilderness,
paths[a] in the desert.

20 The beast of the field will honor Me,
jackals and ostriches;

for I give water in the wilderness,
rivers in the desert, to give drink to My people, My chosen.

21 I have fashioned this people for Me;
they will recount My praise."

THE LORD BLOTS OUT ISRAEL'S TRANSGRESSIONS (43:22–28)

The LORD

22 "But you did not call upon Me, O Jacob,
because you have been weary of Me, O Israel.

23 You have not brought sheep for your burnt offerings to Me,
nor honored Me with your sacrifices;

I have not burdened you with an offering,
nor wearied you with frankincense.

---

a. DSS Isaiah reads "paths" rather than "rivers."

24 You have not bought Me cane with silver,
nor satisfied Me with the fat of your sacrifices,

but you have burdened Me with your sins;
you have wearied Me with your iniquities.

25 I, I am He who blots out your transgressions for My sake,
and I will not remember your sins.

26 Put Me in remembrance. Let us plead together.
Set forth your case so that you will be proved right.

27 Your first father sinned,
and your teachers transgressed against Me.

28 So I profaned the officers of the sanctuary;
let Me give Jacob to destruction
and Israel to reviling."

God Instructs His Covenant People—"You Are My Witnesses" (44:1–8)

The Lord — 44 1 "And now hear, O Jacob, My servant,
and Israel, whom I have chosen."

Isaiah — 2 Thus says the Lord, your Maker,
and your Fashioner from the womb; He will help you.

The Lord — "Do not fear, My servant Jacob
and Jeshurun, whom I have chosen,

3 for I will pour water on the thirsty
and streams on dry ground.

I will pour My Spirit on your seed
and My blessing on your offspring.

4 They will sprout among grass,
like willows beside flowing streams of water.

5 One will say,

Unnamed individual — 'I am the Lord's,'

The Lord — and another will be called by the name of Jacob,
and another will write on his hand,

Written on unnamed individual's hand — 'The Lord's,'

The Lord and he will be called by the name 'Israel.'"

Isaiah [6]Thus says the Lord, the King of Israel
and its Redeemer, and the Lord of Hosts:

The Lord "I am the First,
and I am the Last,

and beside Me there is no god.
[7]And who is like Me?

Let him proclaim,
and let him tell it,
and set it forth for Me;

who has made known the tokens from of old?

Let them tell that which is to come to them.

[8]Do not fear,
nor be afraid.

Have I not announced to you
and declared it from long ago? And you are My witnesses.

Is there a God besides Me?
There is no Rock! I know not any."

The Foolishness of Idolatry (44:9–20)

The Lord [9]"All who fashion an idol are chaos,
and their desirable things will not profit,

and their witnesses do not see,
and they do not know

so that they will be put to shame.
[10]Whoever has fashioned a god or cast an
idol has profited for nothing.

[11]Behold, all that are associated with him will be put to shame,
and the craftsmen, they are but humans.

Let them all assemble;
let them stand up;

they will fear;
they will be put to shame together.

[12]The ironsmith with a tool works it over the coals.
He shapes it with hammers and makes it
with the power of his arm.

Also, he becomes hungry, then there is no strength;
he drinks no water and is faint.

13 The carpenter stretches a line;
he marks the outline with a stylus.

He makes it with planes,
and marks the outline with a compass.

He makes it into the figure of a man,
with the glory of a human, to dwell in a house {temple},

14 cutting down cedars for it,
or taking a cypress, or an oak,

and he lets it grow strong among the trees of the forest.
He plants a cedar, and the rain makes it grow.

15 Then it will be for a human to burn.
He takes part of it and warms himself;
also, he kindles a fire and bakes bread;

also, he makes a god and worships it;
he makes it an idol and bows down before it.

16 Half of it he burns in the fire; over it he roasts meat,
and he eats the meat and is satisfied;

also, he warms himself and says,

Idolater 'Aha, I am warm; I have seen the fire.'

The Lord 17 And the remainder of it he makes into a god,
his idol,

and he falls down before it,
and he worships it,

and he prays to it,
and says,

Idolater 'Save me, for you are my god.'

The Lord 18 They do not know,
nor do they understand;

their eyes are shut so that they cannot see,
their hearts so that they cannot understand.
19 No one takes it to heart,

nor is there knowledge,
nor understanding to say,

Idolater 'Half of it I burned in the fire,

and I baked bread on its coals;
I roasted meat and have eaten.

And the rest of it I will make an abomination;
I will bow down to a block of wood.'

The Lord 20 He feeds on the ashes.

A heart that is deceived has led him astray,
and he cannot save his soul,
and he cannot say,

Idolater 'Is there not a lie in my right hand?'"

The Lord Has Redeemed Israel (44:21–23)

The Lord 21 "Remember these things, O Jacob,
and Israel, for you are My servant.

I have fashioned you; you are My servant.
O Israel, you will not be forgotten by Me.

22 I have wiped clean your transgressions like a thick cloud,
and your sins like a cloud.

Return to Me,
for I have redeemed you."

Isaiah 23 Sing gladly, O heavens, for the Lord has done it.
Shout, O depths of the earth.

Break forth into singing, O mountains,
O forest and every tree in it,

for the Lord has redeemed Jacob,
and He will glorify Himself in Israel.

Cyrus, the Lord's Anointed (44:24–28; 45:1–6)

Isaiah 24 Thus says the Lord, your Redeemer, who fashioned you from the womb,

The Lord "I am the Lord, who made all things,

who alone stretched out the heavens,
who spread out the earth—who was with Me?

25 {I am He} who frustrates the tokens of liars
and makes fools of diviners,

who turns wise men back
and makes their knowledge foolish,

[26]who confirms the word of His servant
and fulfills the counsel of His messengers,

who says of Jerusalem, 'It will be inhabited,'
and the cities of Judah, 'They will be rebuilt,'
and their ruins, 'I will raise them,'

[27]who says to the deep, 'Dry up,
and I will dry up your rivers,'

[28]who says of Cyrus, 'My shepherd,'
and he will fulfill all My purpose,

saying of Jerusalem, 'It will be rebuilt,'
and to the Temple, 'Your foundation will be laid.'"

Isaiah

45 [1]Thus says the Lord to His anointed, to Cyrus,
whose right hand I have grasped,

to subdue nations before him,
and I will loose the loins of kings,

to open double doors before him,
and the gates will not be closed.

The Lord

[2]"I will go before you and level the mountainous land;

I will smash the doors of bronze
and cut through the bars of iron.

[3]I will give you hidden treasures
and the hoards in secret places

so that you may know that I am the Lord,
the God of Israel, who calls you by your name.

[4]For the sake of My servant, Jacob,
and Israel, My chosen,

I called you by your name and gave you a title,
yet you do not know Me.

[5]I am the Lord, and there is no other;
there is no God besides Me.

I gird you,
yet you do not know Me,

6 so that they may know from the rising of the sun
and from the west

that there is none besides Me.
I am the Lord, and there is no other."

The Lord's Supreme Power (45:7–13)

The Lord 7 "I form the light
and create darkness;

I make peace
and create calamity.[a]

I the Lord, do all these things.

8 Shower, O heavens, from above,
and let the skies rain down righteousness;

let the earth open, that salvation may sprout forth,
and let it cause righteousness to spring up together.

I, the Lord, have created it."

Isaiah 9 Woe to him, a potsherd
among the potsherds of the ground,

who strives with his Fashioner.
Does the clay say to its Fashioner,

Clay "What are you making?"
Or "Your work has no hands"?

Isaiah 10 Woe to him, who says to a father,

Unnamed individual "What are you begetting?"

Isaiah Or to a woman,

Unnamed individual "What are you bearing?"

Isaiah 11 Thus says the Lord,
the Holy One of Israel
and its Fashioner:

---

a. Our all-powerful God is in control of all things, including peace and calamity (the Hebrew word *ra'* is sometimes difficult to translate; it can mean "calamity," "evil," "of little worth," "reprobate," etc.).

The Lord

"Ask me concerning things to come;
will you command Me concerning my children
and concerning the work of My hands?

12 I made the earth,
and I have created the human upon it.

It is I; My hands stretched out the heavens,
and commanded all their hosts.

13 It is I; I have aroused him in righteousness,
and I will make straight all his ways;

he will build My city
and set free My exiles,

not for price
nor reward,"

Isaiah

says the Lord of Hosts.

Nations Will Acknowledge the Lord (45:14–17)

Isaiah

14 Thus says the Lord,

The Lord

"The wealth of Egypt, and the merchandise of Cush,
and the Sabeans, people of stature,

will pass over to you and be yours;
they will walk behind you.

They will pass over to you in chains, and bow down to you;
they will make supplications:

People of stature

'Surely God is with you,
and there is none other save God.'"

Isaiah

15 Truly You are a God who hides Yourself,

O God of Israel,
the Savior.

16 All of them are shamed and confounded;
together they walk in confusion, the makers of idols.

17 Israel is saved by the Lord
with an everlasting salvation.

The Lord (to His people)

"You will not be shamed
nor confounded for all eternity."

The Lord Is God of the Whole Earth (45:18–25)

Isaiah

[18] For thus says the Lord, who created the heavens,
He is God, who fashioned the earth

and made it.
He established it;

He did create it—not a chaos—
He formed it to be inhabited.

The Lord

"I am the Lord,
and there is no other.

[19] I did not speak in secret at a place in the land of darkness;
I did not say to the seed of Jacob, 'Seek Me in chaos.'

I, the Lord, speak the truth,
declaring what is right.

[20] Assemble yourselves and come;
draw near, survivors of nations.

They who carry their idol of wood know nothing;
they who pray to a god that cannot save.

[21] Declare and bring it forth.
Let them counsel together.

Who announced this long ago?
Was it not I, the Lord, who declared it of old?

And there is no other God beside Me, a righteous God
and the Savior; there is none besides Me.

[22] Turn to Me and be saved,
all ends of the earth,

for I am God,
and there is no other.

[23] I have sworn by Myself;
righteousness has gone forth from My mouth,
and a word that will not return.

For every knee will bow,
and every tongue will swear to Me.

[24] Moreover, let it be said:

Unnamed individuals

'Only in the Lord are righteousness and strength! To Him will come all who were angry against Him, and they will be ashamed. [25]Through the Lord, all the seed of Israel will become righteous, and they will glory.'"

Idols Have No Power (46:1–7)

Isaiah

46 [1]Bel bows down;
Nebo stoops;

their false gods are carried by beasts of burden;
your loads are borne by weary beasts.

[2]They stoop;
they bow down together.

They cannot deliver the burden,
and they themselves go into captivity.

The Lord

[3]"Hearken to Me, O house of Jacob,
and all the remnant of the house of Israel,
[4]and even to your old age, I am He;
to gray hair, I will carry.

I have made, and I will bear;
I will carry and rescue.

[5]To whom will you liken Me and consider Me equal,
and compare Me that we may be alike?

[6]Those who pour gold from a bag
and weigh silver in the scales,

hire a goldsmith,
and he makes it into a god;

they bow down,
and they worship.

[7]They lift it upon the shoulder;
they carry it.

They set it in its place,
and it stands;
it cannot move from its place.

If [they][a] cry to it,
it does not answer
nor save him from his trouble."

---

a. Bracketed word is from JST.

The Lord Will Accomplish All His Purposes (46:8–13)

The Lord

8"Remember this and stand firm;
take it to heart, O transgressors.
9Remember the former things of old,

for I am God, and there is no other God,
and there is none like Me.

10Declaring the end from the beginning,
and from ancient times, that which has not been done.

Saying, 'My counsel will stand,
and I will do that which I desire.'

11Calling a bird of prey from the east,
a man of My counsel from a far country.

Indeed, I have spoken, I will bring it to pass:
As I have purposed, indeed, I will do it.

12Listen to Me, you stubborn of heart,
you who are far from righteousness.

13I bring My righteousness near;
it is not far off.

And My salvation will not delay.
I will give salvation in Zion, My glory to Israel."

Babylon Will Be Destroyed (47:1–15)

The Lord

47 1"Come down and sit in the dust,
O virgin[a] daughter of Babylon;
sit on the ground without a throne,
O daughter of the Chaldeans,

for they will no longer call you 'tender' and 'delicate.'

2Take the millstones
and grind flour.

Take off your veil,
strip off your robe,
uncover your leg, cross the rivers.

a. Many terms present Babylon as feminine: "virgin" (47:1; is the Lord mocking Babylon with this term?), "daughter" (47:1, 5), "tender and delicate" (47:1), "veil" (47:2), "mistress" (47:5, 7), and "widow" (47:8–9). Additionally, the Hebrew language also uses several feminine verbs, that are lost in the English translation.

[3]Your nakedness will be uncovered;
also, your shame will be seen.

I will take vengeance,
and I will spare no human."

Isaiah [4]Our Redeemer—the Lord of Hosts is His name—
the Holy One of Israel.

The Lord [5]"Sit in silence
and go in darkness,

O daughter of the Chaldeans;
for you will no longer be called

Unnamed individuals 'The Mistress of Kingdoms.'

The Lord [6]I was angry with My people;
I profaned My inheritance,
and I gave them into your hand.

You showed them no mercy.
You made your yoke exceedingly heavy on the aged.

[7]And you said,

Babylon 'I will be a mistress forever.'

The Lord You did not lay these things to heart
or remember the end.

[8]And now listen, you lover of pleasures
who sits securely,
who says in her heart:

Babylon 'I am,
and there is no one besides me.

I will not dwell as a widow
or know the loss of children.'

The Lord [9]These two things will come to you in a moment,
in one day—

the loss of children
and widowhood.

They will come upon you in full measure,
despite your many sorceriesand the power of your great spells.

[10]You have trusted in your wickedness;
you said,

Babylon 'No one sees me.'

The Lord Your wisdom and your knowledge have led you astray,
and in your heart, you said:

Babylon 'I am,
and there is no one besides me.'

The Lord [11]But evil will come upon you;
you will not know its dawn.

And disaster will fall upon you;
you will not be able to make atonement for it,

and catastrophe of which you know nothing
will come upon you suddenly.

[12]Now stand fast in your enchantments
and your many sorceries with which you
have labored since your youth.

Perhaps you may be able to profit;
perhaps you may inspire terror.

[13]You are worn out because of your many advisors.
Let them stand up and save you,

those who divide the heavens,

who gaze at the stars,
who announce month by month what
is about to happen to you.

[14]Behold, they are like stubble; fire consumes them.
They cannot deliver their souls from the power of the flame.

There is no coal for warming oneself,
no light to sit before.

[15]That is all they can do for you—these you have labored with
and merchandised with since your youth.
They wander, each in his own direction.
There is no one to save you."

The Lord Deals with a Stubborn Covenant People (48:1–16)

Isaiah **48** [1][Hearken and][a]
hear this,

O house of Jacob,
who are called by the name of Israel,

---

a. Bracketed items in verses 1–16 set forth the variant readings in 1 Nephi 20:1–16.

who came forth from the waters of Judah
[or out of the waters of baptism],

who swear by the name of the Lord
and acknowledge the God of Israel,

[yet they swear] not in truth
nor in righteousness.

2 [Nevertheless], they call themselves of the holy city,
and they lean upon the God of Israel,

[who is the Lord of Hosts;
yea] the Lord of Hosts is His name.

The Lord 3 ["Behold,] the former things I announced from of old;
and they went forth out of My mouth,

and I announced them.
I did [show] them suddenly, and they came to pass.

4 [I did it] because I knew that you are obstinate,
and your neck is iron sinew,
and your forehead is brass.

5 And I have told you from old;
before it came to pass, I [showed them] to you,
[and I showed them for fear]

lest you should say—

Idolater 'My idol has done them;
my carved and molten images have commanded them.'

The Lord 6 You have [seen and] heard. Now see all this!
And you, will you not declare it?

I announced to you new things from this time,
and hidden things, and you did not know them.

7 They are created now,
and not from the beginning,

and before today you had not heard
[they were declared to you],
lest you should say—

Idolater 'Behold, I knew them.'

The Lord 8 Moreover, you never heard;
moreover, you never knew;
moreover, from that time your ear was not opened,

for I knew that you would certainly betray
and that you were called a transgressor from the womb.

[9] [Nevertheless][a], for My name's sake I will defer My anger;
and for My praise will I hold it back from you,
so as not to cut you off.

[10] Behold, I have refined you, but not with silver;
I have chosen you in the furnace of affliction.

[11] For My sake, [yea],
for My sake will I do it,

for [I will not suffer] my name to be polluted[b],
and My glory I will not give to another.

[12] Hearken to Me, O Jacob,
and Israel, whom I have called;

I am He; I am the first,
and I am also the last.

[13] Indeed, My hand has laid the foundation of the earth,
and My right hand has spread out the heavens.

I call to them;
they stand forth together."

Isaiah [14] All of you, assemble yourselves and hear! Who among them
has declared these things [unto them]? The Lord has loved
him; [yea, and He will fulfil His word that He hath declared
by them;

and] He will do His desire against Babylon,
and His arm [will come upon] the Chaldeans.

[15] [Also, says the Lord:]

The Lord "I, [the Lord, yea,] I have spoken;
yea, I have called him [to declare,]

I have brought him,
and I[c] will make his way prosperous.

[16] Come near to Me;

I have not spoken in secret; from the beginning,
from the time that it was, there I [declared have I spoken."]

---

a. Bracketed items in verses 9–16 are from 1 Nephi 20:9–16.

b. DSS Isaiah reads "I be profaned."

c. One DSS Isaiah scroll reads "I" rather than "he."

Isaiah And the Lord, the Lord
and His Spirit, has sent me.

Blessings God Desired for Israel (48:17–19)

Isaiah 17 [And][a] thus says the Lord,
your Redeemer,
the Holy One of Israel,

The Lord "[I have sent him,] the Lord your God,
who teaches you to avail,
who leads you in the way you should go, [has done it].

18 O that you had hearkened to My commandments—
then your peace would have been like a river,
and your righteousness like the waves of the sea.

19 And your seed also would have been like the sand,
the offspring of your loins like its grain;

their name would never be cut off
or destroyed from before Me."

Song of the Flight from Babylon (48:20–22)

Isaiah 20 Go forth from Babylon;
flee from Chaldea.

With a voice of singing declare,
tell this, send it [voice of singing] to the end of the earth; say,

Singers "The Lord has redeemed His servant, Jacob.
And they did not thirst in the deserts where He led them.

21 He caused the waters to flow out of the rock for them;
He split the rock, and the water gushed out."

Isaiah 22 [And notwithstanding He has done all this,
and greater also,][b] the Lord says:

The Lord "There is no peace for the wicked."

---

a. Bracketed items in verse 17 are from 1 Nephi 20:17.

b. Words in brackets are from 1 Nephi 20:22.

TWO SERVANTS—THE MESSIAH AND THE HOUSE OF ISRAEL (49:1–12)

The LORD (to Israel)

49 1 ["Hearken, O you house of Israel, all you that are broken off and are driven out because of the wickedness of the pastors of My people, yea, all you that are broken off, that are scattered abroad, who are of My people, O house of Israel].[a]

Hear, O islands,
and listen attentively, peoples from afar."

Messiah

"The LORD has called me from the womb;
from my mother's belly, He assigned my name.

2 And He made my mouth like a sharp sword;
He hid me in the shadow of His hand.

And He made me a sharpened arrow;
He hid me in His quiver."

Israel

3 And He {the Lord} said to me,

The LORD

"You are My servant, O Israel, in whom I will glorify myself."

Messiah

4 And I said, "I have labored in vain.
I have spent my strength for chaos and vanity.

Yet my judgment is with the LORD,
and my reward is with my God.

5 And now the LORD said, He who formed me
from the womb as His servant,

to bring Jacob back to Him,
and Israel will be gathered to Him.

And I am honored in the eyes of the LORD,
and my God has become my strength."

6 And He said,

The LORD (to the Messiah)

"It is an easy thing that you should be My servant,
to raise up the tribes of Jacob
and to restore the preserved ones of Israel.

I will make you a light to the nations,
to be My salvation to the ends of the earth."

---

a. Biblical commentators have different views of Isaiah 49:1–12, especially regarding the identification of the speakers and the servants (see verses 3, 5, 6 and 7). But 1 Nephi 21 (see the words in brackets) helps us to identify both the speakers and the recipients of the message. In this section, there are two different servants—the Messiah (see verses 5, 6, 7, and 8) and Israel (see verse 3).

Isaiah

7 Thus says the Lord,
the Redeemer of Israel,
His Holy One,

to the one who is despised,
abhorred by nations, to the servant of rulers:

The Lord

"Kings will see,
and princes will arise.

And they will bow down, because of the Lord, who is faithful,
the Holy One of Israel, and He has chosen you."

Isaiah

8 Thus says the Lord,

The Lord (to the isles)

"In an acceptable time, I have answered
you, [O isles of the sea,][a]
and in a day of salvation, I have helped you.

The Lord (to the Messiah)

And I will preserve you,
and I will make you [My servant] to be
a covenant of the people,

to establish the land,
to cause to inherit desolate inheritances.

9 That you may say to the prisoners,

Messiah

'Go forth,'

The Lord

to those [that sit][b] in darkness,

Messiah

'Show yourselves.'"

Isaiah

They will feed along the ways,
and their pastures will be on all barren heights.

10 They will not hunger
nor will they thirst,

neither will heat
nor [the][c] sun smite them:

for He that has compassion on them will lead them;
even by the springs of water will He guide them.

The Lord

11 And I will make all My mountains a way,
and My highways will be exalted.

---

a. Words in brackets in verse 8 are from 1 Nephi 21:8.

b. Words in brackets are from 1 Nephi 21:9.

c. Word in brackets is from 1 Nephi 21:10.

[12][And then, O house of Israel,][a]
behold, these will come from far:
and behold, these from the north
and from the west;
and these from the land of Sinim."

The Lord Comforts His Returning Children (49:13–21)

Isaiah [13]Sing gladly, O heavens,
and be joyful, O earth;

[for the feet of those who are in the east will be established;
and][b] break forth into singing, O mountains:
[for they will be smitten no more;]

for the Lord has comforted His people
and will have compassion upon His afflicted.

[14]But [behold] Zion says,

Lady Zion "The Lord has forsaken me,
and my Lord has forgotten me"

Isaiah [15][—but He will show that He has not].

The Lord "Can a woman forget her nursing child,
lack compassion on the son of her womb?

Yea, they may forget,
yet I will not forget you, [O house of Israel].

[16]Behold, I have engraved you on the palms of My hands;
your walls are always before Me.

[17]Your children are swift [against] your destroyers,
and they who lay you waste, depart from you.

[18]Lift up your eyes,
and look all around.

All of them gather together;
they will come to you.

[And] as I live,"

Isaiah declares the Lord,

---

a. Words in brackets are from 1 Nephi 21:12.

b. Bracketed words in verses 13–18 are from 1 Nephi 21:13–18.

The Lord “you will surely clothe all of them, as with an ornament,
and bind them on, as a bride.

19 For your waste places,
and your desolate places,
and your destroyed land

will even now be too narrow for inhabitants,
and those who swallowed you up will be far away.

20 The children of your bereavement
will again say in your ears,

Bereaved children ‘The place is too narrow for me;
make place for me that I may dwell.’

The Lord 21 Then will you say in your heart,

Lady Zion ‘Who gave birth for me to these? I was bereaved
and barren, exiled and put away.
And who has brought up these? Behold, I was
left alone; these, where were they?’”

Nations Will Assist Returning Israel (49:22–26)

Isaiah 22 Thus says the Lord:

The Lord “Behold, I will lift My hand to the nations,
and I will raise My ensign to the peoples;

and they will bring your sons in their lap,
and your daughters will be carried upon their shoulders.

23 And kings will be your foster fathers,
and their princesses your wet nurses.

Faces to the ground, they will bow down to you
and lick up the dust of your feet;

then you will know that I am the Lord.
They who wait for Me will not be ashamed.”

24 [For][a] will the prey be taken from the mighty
or captives of a tyrant be rescued?”

Isaiah 25 For thus says the Lord:

The Lord “Even captives of the mighty will be taken away,
and the prey of the tyrant will be rescued.”

---

a. Bracketed word is from 1 Nephi 21:24.

Isaiah For [the Mighty God will deliver His covenant people. For thus says the Lord.][a]

The Lord "I will contend with them that contend with you,
and I will save your children.

26 And I will feed them that oppress you with their own flesh,
and they will be drunk with their own
blood, as with sweet wine;

then all flesh will know that I the Lord
am your Savior
and your Redeemer,
the Mighty One of Jacob."

Israel Is Faithless, Despite God's Power (50:1–3)

Isaiah **50** 1 [Yea, for][b] thus says the Lord,

The Lord ["Have I put you away,
or have I cast you off forever?"

Isaiah For thus says the Lord],

The Lord "Where is the divorce certificate of your mother;
[to] whom I have put [you] away?

Or to which of My creditors did I sell you?
[Yea], to whom have [I] sold you?

Behold, for your iniquities you have been sold,
and for your transgressions your mother was sent away.

2 Why when I come, there was no one there?
I called, [yea][c], there was no answer?

[O house of Israel,][d] is My hand really too short to redeem,
or have I no power to deliver?

Behold, at my rebuke I dry up the sea,
I make [their][e] rivers a wilderness,

---

a. JST textual variation.
b. Bracketed words in verse 1 are from JST and 2 Nephi 7:1.
c. From JST and 2 Nephi 7:2.
d. From JST and 2 Nephi 7:2.
e. From JST.

[and][a] their fish to stink, because [the waters are dried up][b],
and they die because of thirst.

3 I clothe the heavens with blackness,
and I make sackcloth their covering."

Prophecies of the Messiah (50:4–9)

Messiah

4 The Lord, the Lord has given Me the tongue of the learned,
to know how to speak a word in season [unto you,
O house of Israel, when you are][c] weary;

He wakens—morning by morning—
He wakens My ear to hear as do the disciples.

5 The Lord, the Lord has [appointed][d] My ear,

and I was not rebellious,
nor did I turn away backward.

6 I gave My back to the [smiter][e]
and My cheeks to them that plucked My beard.
I hid not My face from insults and spitting.

7 But the Lord, the Lord will help me,
therefore, I will not be confounded;
therefore, have I set My face like flint,
and I know that I will not be ashamed.
8 [And the Lord][f] is near, [and He] justifies me;
who will contend with Me?
Let us stand together!
Who is My adversary? Let him approach Me, [and I
will smite him with the strength of My mouth.]

9 [For][g] the Lord, the Lord will help Me; [and
all they which][h] will condemn Me?

Behold, they all will wear out as a garment,
[and][i] the moth will eat them up.

---

a. From JST and 2 Nephi 7:2.
b. From JST and 2 Nephi 7:2.
c. JST and 2 Nephi 7:4–9 present textual variants.
d. Bracketed word is from JST.
e. From JST and 2 Nephi 7:6.
f. Bracketed words in verse 8 are from JST and 2 Nephi 7:8.
g. Bracketed word is from JST and 2 Nephi 7:9.
h. Bracketed words are from JST and 2 Nephi 7:9.
i. From 2 Nephi 7:9.

The Lord's "Bright Light" Versus Mortal's "Sparks" (50:10–11)

Isaiah

10 Who among you fears the Lord,
obeying the voice of His servant?

Let him that walks in darkness,
and has no bright light,

trust in the name of the Lord
and rely on his God.

11 Behold, all you who kindle fire,
who gird on sparks,

walk in the light of your fire
and in the sparks you have lit.

This will you have of my hand—
you will lie down in sorrow.

The Lord Comforts Zion in the Last Days (51:1–16)

The Lord

51 1 "Listen to Me, you who pursue righteousness,
you who seek the Lord.

Look to the rock from which you were hewn
and to the quarry from which you were cut.

2 Look to Abraham your father
and to Sarah who gave birth to you;

for he was only one when I called him,
then I blessed him, and I multiplied him."

Isaiah

3 For the Lord comforts Zion:
He comforts all her desolate places;

and He will make her wilderness like Eden
and her desert like the garden of the Lord;

exultation and rejoicing will be found in her,
thanksgiving, and the sound of singing.

The Lord

4 "Hearken to Me, My people;
and My nation, give ear to Me;

for the law will go forth from Me,
and I will make My judgment as a light for peoples.

5 My righteousness is near;
My salvation is gone forth,
and My arm will judge peoples;

the isles will hope for Me,
and on My arm, they will wait.

6 Lift up your eyes to the heavens,
and look upon the earth beneath;

for the heavens will vanish like smoke,
and the earth will wear out like a garment,
and they that dwell therein will die in like manner;

but My salvation will be forever,
and My righteousness will never be shattered.

7 Listen to Me, you that know righteousness,
a people in whose heart [I have written][a] My law;

fear not the insults of men,
neither be dismayed at their revilings,

8 for the moth will eat them like a garment,
and the worm will eat them like wool;

but My righteousness will be forever,
and My salvation from generation to generation."

Isaiah 9 Awake, awake! Clothe yourself with strength;
O arm of the Lord, awake, as in the days of old.

Are you [He][b] that cut Rahab to pieces?
Piercing the sea monster?

10 Are you not [He][c] that has dried the sea,
the waters of the great deep,
that has made a way in the depths of the sea
for the redeemed to pass over?

11 And the ransomed of the Lord will return
and come with singing to Zion;

and everlasting joy [and holiness][d] will be upon their heads,
[and][e] gladness and joy will overtake them;
sorrow and sighing will flee away.

---

a. From JST and 2 Nephi 8:7.
b. From 2 Nephi 8:9.
c. From 2 Nephi 8:10
d. From JST and 2 Nephi 8:11.
e. From 2 Nephi 8:11.

The Lord

[12]"I [am He,
yea][a], I am He,

who comforts you.
[Behold], who are you,

that you are afraid of a man that will die,
and of a son of a human, who is made like grass?

[13]And you forgot the Lord,
your Maker,

who stretches out the heavens
and lays the foundations of the earth;

and you have feared continually every day
because of the fury of the oppressor,
when he sets himself to destroy? And where
is the fury of the oppressor?

[14]The one who is captive will quickly be freed
and will not die in the pit,
nor will his bread fail.

[15]And I am the Lord your God, who stirs up the sea
and its waves roar. The Lord of Hosts is His name.

[16]And I have put My words in your mouth,
and I have covered you with the shadow of My hand,

to plant the heavens,
and to lay the foundations of the earth,

and to say to Zion:
'[Behold][b], you are My people.'"

God's Wrath on Jerusalem (51:17–23)

Isaiah

[17]Wake yourself, wake yourself;[c]
arise, O Jerusalem!

You who have drunk from the hand of the Lord,
the cup of His fury;
you have drunk
the dregs of the cup of trembling, drained out.

---

a. Bracketed items in verse 12 are from JST and 2 Nephi 8:12.

b. From JST and 2 Nephi 8:16.

c. JST and 2 Nephi 8:17–25 present textual variants.

[18] [And][a] there is no one guiding her among
all the children she has borne;
and there is no one taking her by the hand, among
all the children she has brought up.

[19] These two [sons] have come to you.
Who will be sorry for you?

[Your] desolation and destruction,
and famine and sword!

[And] who will comfort you?

[20] Your sons have fainted [save these two],
they lie at the head of all the streets;

as an antelope in a net, they are full of the fury of the Lord,
the rebuke of your God.

[21] Therefore hear now this, you afflicted
and drunken, and not with wine.

[22] Thus says Your Lord,
the Lord and Your God,
He who pleads the cause of His people.

The Lord "Behold, I have taken out of your hand the cup of trembling,
the dregs of the cup of My fury; you will not drink it again.

[23] But I will put it into the hand of them that
torment you, who have said to your soul,

Tormenters 'Bow, that we may pass over';

The Lord and you have made your back like the ground
and like the street to them that passed over."

Zion Will Return and Be Redeemed in the Last Days (52:1–12)

The Lord 52 [1] "Awake, awake! Put on your strength, O Zion;
put on your glorious garments,
O Jerusalem, the holy city,

for the uncircumcised
and the unclean will no longer come into you.

[2] Shake yourself from the dust; arise, sit down, O Jerusalem;
loose yourself from the bonds of your neck,
O captive daughter of Zion."

a. Bracketed words in verses 18–20 are from JST and 2 Nephi 8:18–20.

Isaiah 3 For thus says the LORD,

The LORD "You were sold for nothing,
and you will be redeemed without money."

Isaiah 4 For thus says the Lord,

The LORD "At first My people went down to Egypt to live there,
and the Assyrian oppressed them without cause.

5 And now, what have I here,"

Isaiah declares the LORD,

The LORD "that My people are taken away for nothing? They
that rule over them make them to wail,"

Isaiah declares the LORD,

The LORD "and My name continually,
all day, is despised.

6 Therefore my people will know My name;
[yea][a], in that day that [they will know that][b],

it is I who speaks,
'Here I am.'"

7 [And then will they say][c],

God's covenant people "How beautiful upon the mountains are the feet of
him who brings good tidings [unto them],
who announces peace,
who brings good tidings [unto them] of good,
who announces salvation,
who says to Zion,

Herald 'Your God reigns!'"

Isaiah 8 Your watchmen will lift their voice;
with the voice together will they sing gladly:
for they will see eye to eye, when the LORD returns to Zion.

9 Break forth, sing together, O ruins of Jerusalem:

for the LORD has comforted His people;
He has redeemed Jerusalem.

---

a. From JST.
b. From JST and 23 Nephi 20:39.
c. Bracketed words in verse 7 are from JST and 3 Nephi 20:40.

[10]The Lord has made bare His holy arm
in the eyes of all the nations,
and all the ends of the earth will see the salvation of our God.

[11]Depart,
depart;

go out from there; touch not that which is unclean.
Go out from her midst. Be clean, you who
bear the vessels of the Lord.

[12]For you will not go out with haste,
nor will you go by flight;

for the Lord will go before you,
and the God of Israel will be Your rearguard.

The Suffering of the Servant (52:13–15)

The Lord

[13]"Behold, My servant will act wisely;

He will be exalted
and lifted up
and be very high.

[14]So many were astonished at You—

so, His appearance was disfigured[a] more than any man,
and His form more than the children of a human.

[15]So will He [gather][b] many nations; the kings
will shut their mouths because of Him:

for that which had not been told them, they will see;
and that which they have not heard, they will consider."

Suffering and Triumph of the Messiah (53:1–12)

Christ's disciples

53 [1]Who has believed our report?
And to whom has the arm of the Lord been revealed?

---

a. The Hebrew word *mischat*, translated "disfigured," is rare in the Hebrew Bible; it refers to Jesus Christ's disfigurement after he wore the crown of thorns, was beaten and slugged in the face (Matt. 26:67; 27:30), suffered for about three hours in Gethsemane, and experienced the cruelty of the cross. No individual, ever, in eternity, had suffered in such an extreme manner! Thus, Isaiah prophesied, "His appearance was disfigured *more than any man*, and His form *more than the children* of a human" (emphasis added). DSS Isaiah possibly reads "I have anointed his appearance," but this reading is incorrect.

b. JST 52:15 reads "gather."

Isaiah	2 For He will grow up before Him as a tender plant and as a root out of dry ground.
Non-believers	He has no form or majesty that we should look at Him and no appearance that we should desire Him.
Isaiah	3 He is despised and rejected of men, a man of pains and familiar with sickness, and like one from whom people hid their faces. He is despised!
Non-believers	But we esteemed Him not.
Christ's disciples	4 Surely He has borne our sicknesses and carried our pains;
Non-believers	But we esteemed Him stricken, smitten by God, and afflicted.
Christ's disciples	5 But He was pierced for our transgressions; He was crushed for our iniquities. The chastening upon Him made us whole, and with His stripes we are healed.
Non-believers	6 All we like sheep have gone astray; we have turned, each of us, to his own way.
Christ's disciples	And the Lord has laid on Him the [iniquities][a] of us all.
Isaiah	7 He was oppressed, and He was afflicted, but He opened not His mouth. He is brought as a lamb to the slaughter, and as an ewe lamb before her shearers is dumb, He opened not His mouth. 8 He was taken from oppression and from judgment. And who will consider His generation? Because He was cut off out of the land of the living; He was stricken for the [transgressions][b] of my people.

a. From Mosiah 14:4.

b. From Mosiah 14:8.

[9]And He made His grave with the wicked
and with the rich in His death,

though He had done no [evil][a],
nor was any deceit in His mouth.

[10]And the Lord desired to crush Him;
He made Him sick.[b]
When you will make His soul a guilt
offering, He will see His seed,
He will prolong His days,
and the will of the Lord will prosper in His hand.

[11]He will see the trouble of His soul, and He will be satisfied;
by His knowledge, My servant, the Righteous
One, will make many righteous,
and He will bear their iniquities.

The Lord [12]"Therefore, I will divide for Him a portion with the great,
and with the strong He will divide the spoil,

because He has laid His soul bare to death,
and He was numbered with the transgressors;

and He bore the [sins][c] of many
and made intercession for the transgressors."

Zion and Her Stakes Established in the Last Days (54:1–17)

The Lord 54 [1]"Sing gladly, O barren[d] one, who has not given birth;
break forth into singing and cry aloud,
who did not labor with child;

for more are the children of the desolate
than the children of the married wife,"

Isaiah says the Lord.

The Lord [2]"Enlarge the place of your tent,
and let the curtains of your habitations be stretched out.

Do not hold back; lengthen your cords
and strengthen your stakes.

a. From Mosiah 14:9.
b. DSS Isaiah reads, "he pierced him."
c. From Mosiah 14:12.
d. In the Hebrew language, many of the grammatical forms in this chapter are feminine, referring to Lady Zion, though these forms are lost in the translation.

[3]For you will break forth on the right and on the left;
and your seed will take possession of the nations
and will populate the desolate cities.

[4]Fear not, for you will not be ashamed;
and be not confounded, for you will not be put to shame;

for you will forget the shame of your youth,
and you will not remember the dishonor
of your widowhood anymore.

[5]For Your Maker is your Husband;
the LORD of Hosts is His name,

and your Redeemer,
the Holy One of Israel,
the God of the whole earth,
will He be called.

[6]For the LORD has called you, as a wife
forsaken and grieved in spirit,
and a wife of youth, when you were refused,"

Isaiah says your God.

The LORD [7]"For a small moment, I forsook you,
but with great mercies, I will gather you.

[8]In a flood of wrath I hid my face from you for a moment,
but with everlasting loving-kindness I will
have compassion on you,"

Isaiah says the LORD your Redeemer.

The LORD [9]"For this to Me like the waters of Noah,
for I swore that the waters of Noah should
no longer go over the earth;
so, I swore that I would not be angry with you nor rebuke you.

[10]For the mountains will depart,
and the hills will totter,

but My loving-kindness will not depart from you,
nor will the covenant of My [people][a] totter,"

Isaiah says the LORD, who has compassion on you.

The LORD [11]"O afflicted female,
tossed with tempest, not comforted!

---

a. JST 54:10 attests "people" rather than "peace."

Behold, I will set your stones with antimony,
and lay your foundations with sapphires[a],

[12]and make your battlements of rubies,
and your gates of beryl,
and all your walls of precious stones."

[13]And all your children will be taught of the Lord,
and great will be the peace of your children.

[14]In righteousness you will be established.

Keep far from oppression, for you will not fear,
and from terror, for it will not come near you.

[15]"Behold, if anyone will surely stir up strife [against you][b],
it is not of Me;
whoever will stir up strife against you
will fall for your sake.

[16]Behold, I have created the smith that blows the fire of coals
and who brings forth a tool for his work;
and I have created the destroyer to destroy.

[17]No weapon that is formed against you will prosper,
and every tongue that will rise against you in
judgment you will declare guilty.

This is the inheritance of the servants of the Lord,
and their righteousness is of Me,"

Isaiah declares the Lord.

Come to Jehovah, the Living Waters (55:1–5)

The Lord

55 [1]"Everyone who is thirsty,
come to the waters,

and whoever has no silver, come buy and eat;
and come buy wine and milk without silver and without price.

[2]Why do you spend your silver for that which is not bread
and your labor for that which does not satisfy?

Listen carefully to Me, and eat what is good,
and let your soul delight itself in fatness.

---

a. Hebrew, *sappir* may be a sapphire or lapis lazuli—the Hebrew word is rare and difficult to translate

b. Bracketed words are from JST and 3 Nephi 22:15.

3 Stretch your ear and come to Me.
Hear, that your soul may live,

and I will make an everlasting covenant with you—
the sure loving-kindnesses of David.

4 Surely I made him a witness to the peoples,
a leader and commander of the peoples.

5 Surely you will call a nation that you know not,
and a nation that did not know you will run to you,

for the sake of the LORD, your God,
and for the Holy One of Israel, for He has glorified you."

SEEK THE LORD AND FORSAKE OUR WICKED WAYS (55:6–13)

Isaiah

6 Seek the LORD while He may be found;
call upon Him while He is near.

7 Let the wicked forsake his way,
and the unrighteous man his thoughts.

Let him return to the LORD,
    and He will have compassion on him,
and to our God,
    for He will abundantly forgive.

The LORD

8 "For My thoughts are not your thoughts,
neither are your ways My ways,"

Isaiah

declares the LORD.

The LORD

9 "For as the heavens
are higher than the earth,

so, My ways are higher than your ways,
and My thoughts than your thoughts.

10 For as the rain and the snow come down from heaven
and do not return there, but water the earth

making it bring forth and sprout,

and giving seed to the sower
and bread to the one who eats,

11 so My word will be that goes forth from My mouth;
it will not return to Me empty,

but it will accomplish that which I purpose
and will succeed for which I sent it.

[12]For with rejoicing you will go out
and be led with peace;

the mountains and hills will break forth before you in singing,
and all the trees of the field will clap their hands.

[13]Instead of the thorn, the cypress will come up;
instead of the briar, the myrtle will come up."

Isaiah And it will be to the Lord for a name;
for an everlasting sign, it will not be cut off.

The Nations Are Welcomed to God's Covenant (56:1–8)

Isaiah **56** [1]Thus says the Lord,

The Lord "Guard justice
and do righteousness.

For soon My salvation will come,
and My righteousness will be revealed.

[2]Blessed is the man who does this,
and the son of a human who holds it fast,

who keeps the Sabbath and does not profane it,
and keeps his hand from doing any evil."

Isaiah [3]Let not the foreigner[a] who has joined himself to the Lord say,

Foreigner "Surely the Lord will exclude me from His people."

Isaiah And let not the eunuch say,

Eunuch "Behold, I am a dry tree.'"

Isaiah [4]For thus says the Lord:

The Lord "To the eunuchs who guard My Sabbaths,
who choose the things that please Me
and hold fast to My covenant,

[5]I will give to them in My House and within
My walls a hand and a name,
better than sons and daughters;
I will give them an everlasting name that will not be cut off.

a. "Foreigner" here is a technical term (*nekhar* in biblical Hebrew), meaning one who is not part of the house of Israel.

[6]And the foreigners who join themselves to the Lord,
who serve Him,
who love the name of the Lord,
and who are His servants,

everyone who keeps the Sabbath,
and does not profane it,
and holds fast to My covenant,

[7]these I will bring to My Holy Mountain
and make them rejoice in My House of Prayer.

Their burnt offerings
and their sacrifices will be accepted on My altar,

for My House will be called
'A House of Prayer' for all peoples."

Isaiah [8]The Lord, the Lord, who gathers the
outcasts of Israel, declares:

The Lord "I will gather others to it
besides those already gathered."

Israel's Gross Wickedness (56:9–12; 57:1–13a)

Isaiah [9]All beasts of the field, come to eat,
all you beasts in the forest.

[10]His watchmen are all of them blind;
they do not know,

they are all mute dogs,
they cannot bark,

dreaming, lying down, loving to slumber.

[11]And the dogs have a mighty appetite;
they never have enough,

and they are shepherds that have no understanding;
they all have turned to their own way,

each to his own gain,
one and all.

Wicked leaders [12]"Come, let me take wine,
and let us fill ourselves with strong drink.

And tomorrow will be like today,
or even better."

Isaiah

57 [1]The righteous perish,
but no one takes it to heart;
devout people are taken away,
while no one understands
that the righteous man is taken away from evil.

[2]He will enter into peace;
they will rest on their beds, he who walks with uprightness.

The Lord

[3]"But you, draw near, children of the sorceress,
offspring of the adulterer and the prostitute.

[4]Against whom are you making sport?
Against whom do you open wide your
mouth and put out your tongue?

Are you not children of transgression,
the offspring of lies?

[5]You burn with lust among the oaks,
under every leafy tree,

who sacrifice your children in the wadis,
under the clefts of the rocks.

[6]Your portion is in sections of the wadi;
they, they are your destiny.

Also, to them you have poured out a drink offering;
you have brought a cereal offering.

Will I be appeased for these things?

[7]Upon a high and lofty mountain you have set your bed,
and there you went up to offer sacrifice.

[8]Behind the door and the door post you have set up your memorial. Far removed from Me you have uncovered yourself, and you have gone up and made wide your bed. And you have made a covenant for yourself with them. You have loved their bed; you have seen their nakedness.

[9]You journeyed to Molech with oil
and multiplied your perfumes;

you sent your envoys far away
and sent them down, even to Sheol.[a]

[10]You were wearied with the greatness of your way;
you did not say,

---

a. On the meaning of the Hebrew word *sheol*, see Isaiah 5:14, footnote a.

The wicked ‘It is hopeless.’

The Lord You found renewal for your power;
therefore, you did not faint.

11 Whom did you dread
and fear, so that you lied

and did not remember Me,
nor did you lay it to heart?

Have I not held my peace for a long time,
and you did not fear Me?

12 I will declare your righteousness
and your works,

but they will not profit you.
When you cry out, let your group of idols[a] deliver you;

13 the wind will lift all of them,
a breath will take them away.”

Blessings for the Righteous (57:13b–21)

The Lord 13 “But he who takes refuge in Me will possess the land
and will inherit My holy mountain.”

Isaiah 14 And He will say,

The Lord “Build up,
build up the road[b],

prepare the way;
lift the stumbling block from My people’s way.”

Isaiah 15 For thus says the High and Lofty One, who inhabits eternity,
whose name is “Holy,”

The Lord “I dwell in the high and holy place

and with the contrite and lowly in spirit,
reviving the lowly in spirit and reviving
the hearts of the contrite.

16 For I will not contend forever,
nor will I always be angry,

---

a. The Hebrew reads *qibbutz*, literally has “collection” or “assemblage,” but some commentators hold that the text implies a collection of idols, so “of idols” is added to the translation.

b. “road” [Hebrew, *msilla*] is from DSS Isaiah

because the spirit would grow faint before Me,
and the souls that I have made.

17 I was angry at the iniquity of his covetousness.
I smote him, hiding, and I was angry,
but he went on backsliding in the way of his own heart.

18 I have seen his ways, but I will heal him;
I will lead him and restore comforts to
him and to his mourners,

19 creating the fruit of the lips.
Peace, peace, to those far and near,"

Isaiah says the Lord,

The Lord "and I will heal him.

20 But the wicked are like the tossing sea, for it cannot be quiet,
and its waters toss up mire and dirt.
21 There is no peace for the wicked,"

Isaiah says my God.

The True Law of the Fast (58:1–12)

The Lord to Isaiah

58 1 "Cry aloud, spare not,
lift your voice like a ram's horn,

and tell My people their transgression,
the house of Jacob their sin.

2 And Me, they seek daily
and delight to know My ways,

as if they were a nation that did righteousness
and did not forsake their God's justice.

They ask Me for righteous judgments;
they delight to approach God.

God's covenant people

3 'Why have we fasted, when You did not see it?
Why have we afflicted our soul, when You did not know it?'

The Lord

"Behold, in the day of your fast you found pleasure,
and you oppress all your workers.

4 Behold, you fast to quarrel and to fight
and to smite with a fist of wickedness;

you will not fast as such on this day,
to make your voice heard on high.

[5]Is that the sort of fast that I choose?
Is it a day for a human to afflict his soul?

Is it to bow down his head like a reed and
to spread sackcloth and ashes?
Will you call this fast an acceptable day to the Lord?

[6]Is this not the fast that I choose:
to open the bonds of wickedness,
to undo the straps of the yoke,

to let the oppressed go free,
and to break every yoke?

[7]Is it not sharing your bread with the hungry,
bringing the homeless poor into your house?

When you see the naked, covering him?
And from your own flesh, you will not hide yourself?"

Isaiah [8]Then will your light break forth like the dawn,
and your healing will speedily sprout up.

Your righteousness will go before you;
the glory of the Lord will be your rearguard.

[9]Then you will call, and the Lord will answer;
then you will cry for help, and He will say,

The Lord "Here I am."

Isaiah If you remove the yoke from among you,
the pointing finger, and speaking wickedness,

[10]if you pour out your soul for the hungry
and satisfy the desire of the afflicted,

then your light in the dark will rise as the sun,
and your darkness will be as the noonday.

[11]And the Lord will guide you continually,

and satisfy your soul while in scorched places,
and make your bones strong.

You will be like a watered garden,
like a source of water whose waters do not fail.

[12]And some of you will rebuild ancient ruins.
You will raise up the foundations of many generations.

You will be called,

Titles of one who properly fasts

“The Repairer of the Broken Walls,”
“The Restorer of Paths to Dwell in.”

Blessings of the Sabbath (58:13–14)

The Lord

13 “If you turn away your foot from the Sabbath,
from doing your pleasure on My holy day,

and call the Sabbath: ‘Delight,’
‘the Holy of the Lord,’ ‘Honorable,’

and you will honor it by not going your own ways,
nor finding your own pleasure,
nor speaking idly,

14 then you will take delight in the Lord,
and I will make you ride upon the heights of the earth,
and I will feed you the inheritance of Jacob, your father,”

Isaiah

for the mouth of the Lord has spoken.

Iniquities Separate the Wicked from God (59:1–15a)

Isaiah

59 1 Behold, the hand of the Lord is not shortened,
that it cannot save,
nor His ear too dull,
that it cannot hear.

2 But your iniquities have caused a separation
between you and your God,
and your sins have hidden His face
from you so that He does not hear.

3 For your palms are defiled with blood,
and your fingers with iniquity;

your lips have spoken lies,
your tongue mutters wickedness.

4 No one calls for righteousness,
and no one pleads honestly;

they rely on chaos,
and they speak lies;

they conceive mischief
and give birth to iniquity.

[5] They hatch the eggs of venomous snakes;
and they weave the web of spiders.

Whoever eats their eggs will die,
and if one is broken, a viper is hatched.

[6] Their webs will not become garments;
men will not cover themselves with their works.

Their works are works of iniquity,
and deeds of violence are in their palms.

[7] Their feet run to evil,
and they are quick to shed innocent blood.

Their thoughts are thoughts of iniquity.
Desolation and destruction are in their paths.

[8] They know not the road of peace,
and there is no justice in their roadways.

They have made their pathways crooked for themselves;
whoever walks in them does not know peace.

Wicked

[9] Therefore, justice is far from us,
and righteousness does not overtake us.

We wait for light, but behold darkness,
for brightness, but we walk in gloom.

[10] We grope for the wall like the blind;
and we grope like those who have no eyes.

We stumble at noon as if it were twilight,
among the healthy, like dead men.

[11] We all growl like bears;
indeed, we moan like doves.

We wait for justice, but there is none,
for salvation, but it is far from us.

[12] For our transgressions are multiplied before You,
and our sins testify against us;

for our transgressions are with us,
and our iniquities—we know them.

[13] Transgressing and lying against the Lord
and turning away from following our God,

speaking oppression and revolt,
conceiving and uttering lying words from the heart.

[14]And justice is turned back,
and righteousness stands far away,

because truth has stumbled in the public square,
and uprightness cannot enter.

[15]Truth is lacking,
and he who departs from evil makes himself a prey.

Salvation for the Righteous, Vengeance for the Wicked (59:15b–21)

Isaiah

[15]The Lord saw it,
and it was displeasing in His eyes that there was no justice.

[16]And He saw that there was no man,
and He was appalled that there was no one to intervene;

then His own arm brought Him salvation,
and His righteousness upheld Him.

[17]He clothed Himself with righteousness as a breastplate,
and upon His head a helmet of salvation.

He clothed Himself with garments of vengeance for clothing
and wrapped Himself in zeal as a robe.

[18]According to their deeds so will He pay,
wrath to His adversaries,
recompense to His enemies; He will pay
recompense to the islands.

[19]So they will fear the name of the Lord from the west,
and His glory from the rising of the sun,

and He will come like a surging river,
which the Spirit of the Lord drives on.

The Lord [20]"And the Redeemer will come to Zion,
to those in Jacob who turn from transgression,"

Isaiah declares the Lord.

The Lord [21]"And as for Me, this is My covenant with them,"

Isaiah says the Lord:

The Lord "My Spirit, which is upon you,

and My words, which I have put in your mouth,
will not depart from of your mouth,

nor out of the mouth of your seed,
nor out of the mouth of your seed's seed,
from this time and forever,"

Isaiah says the LORD.

THE GLORY OF ZION IN THE LAST DAYS (60:1–22)

Isaiah 60 [1]Arise,
shine,

for your light has come,
and the glory of the LORD has risen upon you.

[2]For behold, the darkness will cover the earth,
and thick darkness the people,

but the LORD will arise on you,
and His glory will appear on you.

[3]And nations will go to your light,
and kings to the brightness of your rising.

[4]Lift up your eyes around you
and see:

they all gather together;
they come to you—

your sons will come from a distance,
and your daughters will be supported on your side.

[5]Then you will see and be radiant;
your heart will be in awe and grow large,

because the abundance of the sea will be turned over to you,
the wealth of nations will come to you.

[6]A multitude of camels will cover you;
the young camels of Midian, of Ephah,
all from Sheba will come,

They will carry gold and frankincense,
and they will bear good news, the praises of the LORD.

[7]All the flocks of Kedar will be gathered to you;
the rams of Nebaioth will serve you.

The LORD "They will come up, with acceptance, on My altar.
I will glorify My glorious House.

[8]Who are these that fly like a cloud,
and like doves to their dovecotes?

[9]Surely the islands will wait for Me."

Isaiah

First, the ships of Tarshish, bringing your
children from a distance,
with their silver and their gold,

unto the name of the Lord your God,
and for the Holy One of Israel,
because He has glorified you.

[10]And foreigners will build up your walls,
and their kings will serve you.

The Lord

"For in my wrath, I smote you,
but in My favor, I show you compassion.

[11]And your gates will be open continually;
they will not be shut day and night,

that they may bring the wealth of the nations to you,
with their kings led in procession.

[12]For the nation and the kingdom
that will not serve you will perish,
and the nations
will certainly be laid waste.

[13]The glory of Lebanon will come to you—
the cypress, the plane, and the pine together—

to beautify the place of My sanctuary,
and I will make glorious the place of My feet.

[14]The children of those who oppressed you
will come bending low to you,
and all who despised you
will bow down at your feet;

and they will call you,"

Former oppressors

'The City of the Lord,'
'The Zion of the Holy One of Israel.'

The Lord

[15]"Whereas you have been forsaken
and hated, with no one passing through,

I will make you majestic forever,
an exultation from generation to generation.

16You will suck the milk of nations,
and the breast of kings you will suck,

and you will know that I, the Lord, am your Savior
and your Redeemer, the Mighty One of Jacob.

17Instead of bronze, I will bring gold,
and in place of iron, I will bring silver,

and instead of wood, bronze,
and instead of stones, iron.

I will make peace your overseers
and righteousness your taskmasters.

18Violence will no longer be heard in your land,
nor devastation or destruction within your borders,

but you will call your walls"

Zion's inhabitants 'Salvation,'

The Lord and your gates

Zion's inhabitants 'Praise.'

Isaiah 19The sun will no longer be your light by day,
nor will the brightness of the moon give light to you by night[a],

but the Lord will be your everlasting light
and your God your glory.

20Your sun will go down no more,
nor your moon wane,

for the Lord will be your everlasting light.

And the days of your mourning will end.

The Lord 21"Then your people, all of them righteous,
will possess the earth forever,

the shoot of My planting,
the work of My hands, that I might be glorified.

22The little one will become a thousand,
and the small one a strong nation.

I am the Lord;
I will hasten it in [My][b] time."

---

a. DSS Isaiah and LXX has "by night."

b. Bracketed word is from JST.

The Mission of the Messiah (61:1–3)

Messiah

61 [1]"The Spirit of the Lord is upon Me,
because the Lord has anointed Me

to bring good news to the poor;
He has sent Me to bind up the brokenhearted,

to proclaim liberty to the captives
and the opening of the prison to those who are bound;

[2]to proclaim the year of favor of the Lord
and the day of vengeance of our God;

to comfort all who mourn,
to grant to those who mourn in Zion;

[3]to give to them a crown of beauty, instead of ashes;
the oil of gladness, instead of mourning;
a garment of praise, instead of a faint spirit;

that they may be called 'Oaks of Righteousness,'
'the Planting of the Lord,' that He may be glorified."

Blessings to Restored Israel (61:4–11)

The Lord

[4]"They will build up the ancient ruins;
they will raise up the devastated places of old,

and they will repair the ruined cities
and the devastated places of many generations.

[5]And strangers will stand and shepherd your flocks,
and foreigners will be your farmers and your vinedressers.

[6]But you will be called, 'The Priests of the Lord';
they will say of you, 'The Ministers of Our God.'

You will eat the wealth of nations,
and you will boast in their glory.

[7]Instead of your shame, a double portion,
and instead of dishonor, they will sing gladly in your portion.

Therefore, you will possess a double portion in their land;
everlasting rejoicing will be yours.

[8]For I, the Lord, love justice;
I hate robbery by injustice.

I reward you in truth,
and I will make an everlasting covenant with you.

9And your seed will be known among the nations,
and your offspring among the peoples."

Isaiah All who see them will acknowledge them,
that they are a seed whom the Lord has blessed.

The righteous 10I will greatly exult in the Lord;
my soul is joyful in my God,

for He has clothed me with garments of salvation—
He has covered me with a robe of righteousness,

as a bridegroom serves as a priest, with a headdress[a],
and as a bride is adorned with her jewels[b].

11For as the earth brings forth its shoots
and a garden causes seeds to spring up,

so, the Lord, the Lord, will cause righteousness
and praise to spring up before all the nations.

Zion Is Established in the Last Days (62:1–12)

The Lord 62 1"For the sake of Zion, I will not keep silent.
And for the sake of Jerusalem, I will not be quiet,

until her righteousness goes forth as brightness
and her salvation as a burning torch."

Isaiah 2And nations will see your righteousness
and all kings your glory.

And you will be called by a new name,
which the mouth of the Lord will name.

3You will be a crown of glory in the hand of the Lord
and a royal diadem in the palm of your God.

4You will no more be called "Forsaken,"
and your land will no more be called "Desolate,"

because you will be called "[Delightful][c],"
and your land "[Union],"

---

a. The Hebrew term *pe'er* ("headdress") pertains to a special, sacred head covering for a male.

b. The Hebrew term *kele* ("jewels") is a generic term which can refer to ornaments, jewels, and even garments (see the lexicons); hence, the translation can also read, "bride is adorned with her garments," speaking of special clothing.

c. Bracketed words in verse 4 are from JST.

for the Lord delights in you,
and your land will be married.

5 For as a young man marries a virgin,
so will your [God][a] marry you,

and as a bridegroom rejoices over the bride,
so will your God rejoice over you.

The Lord 6 "I have set watchmen upon your walls, O Jerusalem,
and all day and night they will not be silent."

Isaiah Those who mention the Lord do not keep quiet

7 and give no silence to Him until He establishes,
and until He makes Jerusalem the praise in the earth.

8 The Lord has sworn by His right hand,
and by His mighty arm,

The Lord "I will not give your grain for food to your enemies again,
and foreigners will not drink your new wine
for which you have labored.

9 But those who harvest it will eat it and praise the Lord,
and those who gather it will drink it in
the courts of My temple."[b]

Isaiah 10 Pass through, pass through the gates;
prepare the way for the people.

Build up, build up the highway,
clear away the rock,
lift an ensign over the peoples.

11 Behold, the Lord has proclaimed to the end of the earth,
say to the daughter of Zion,

God's covenant people "Behold, your Salvation comes!
Behold, His reward is with Him,
and His recompense is before Him."

Isaiah 12 And they will be called,

Titles of Lord's people "The Holy People,"
"The Redeemed of the Lord."

Isaiah And you will be called,

---

a. Word in brackets is from JST.

b. The Hebrew word can also be translated "holiness" (see KJV); the ESV reads "sanctuary."

Titles of Lady Zion — "Sought After,"
"A City Not Forsaken."

THE LORD'S RED APPAREL AT HIS SECOND COMING (63:1–6)

Unnamed individual(s)

63 1 Who is this who comes from Edom,
with dyed-red garments from Bozrah?

He that is glorious in His apparel,
traveling in the greatness of His strength?

The LORD

"It is I, speaking in righteousness,
mighty to save."

Unnamed individual(s)

2 Why is Your apparel red
and Your garments like him that treads in the wine press?

The LORD

3 "I have trodden the wine press alone,
and no one was with Me from the people.

I did tread upon them in My anger
and trampled them in My fury,

and their lifeblood spattered on My garments,
and I have stained all My apparel.

4 For the day of vengeance was in My heart,
and the year of My redeemed has come.

5 I looked, but there was no one to help;
I was appalled, but there was no one to uphold.

So, My arm brought salvation to Me,
and My wrath upheld Me.

6 I trampled down peoples in My anger,
I made them drunk in My wrath,
and I poured out their lifeblood on the earth."

PSALM OF THE LORD'S LOVING-KINDNESSES (63:7–14)

Worshipper

7 I will recount the loving-kindnesses of the LORD,
the praises of the LORD,

according to all that the LORD has granted us,
the many good things to the house of Israel,

which He has granted them according to His mercy
and according to the abundance of His loving-kindnesses.

8 For He said,

The Lord “Surely, they are My people,
children who will not deal falsely.”

Isaiah And He became their Savior!

9 In all their affliction,
He was afflicted,

and the angel of His presence saved them.
In His love and in His pity, He redeemed them.

He bore them
and carried them all the days of old.

10 But they rebelled
and grieved His Holy Spirit,

and He turned and became their enemy,
and He fought against them.

11 But he [Israel] remembered the days of old—
Moses and his people!

Where is He who brought them up out of the
sea with the shepherds of His flock?
Where is He who put His Holy Spirit in the midst of them?

12 Who led them by the right hand of Moses
with His glorious arm,

who divided the waters before them
to make for Himself an everlasting name,
13 who led them through the depths?

Like a horse in the wilderness, that they did not stumble,
14 like cattle that go down into the valley,

the Spirit of the Lord gave them rest,
so, You led Your people to make a glorious name for Yourself.

A Prayer Addressing, “O Lord” (63:15–19; 64:1–12)

Isaiah? God’s servants? 15 Look from heaven,
and see from Your holy and glorious habitation.

Where is Your zeal,
and Your might,

the yearning of Your inner parts,
and Your compassion? They are withheld from me.

[16]For You are our Father,
though Abraham does not know us,
and Israel does not acknowledge us;
You, O LORD, are our Father,

our Redeemer;
Your name is everlasting.

[17]O LORD, why have You [suffered][a] us
to wander from Your ways
and [to harden] our heart from your fear?

Return, for the sake of Your servants,
the tribes of Your inheritance.

[18]For a brief time Your holy people had possession;
our adversaries trampled down Your Temple.

[19]We have become like those You have never ruled,
those who are not called by Your name.

64 [1]O, that You would rend the heavens,
that You would come down so that the
mountains would flow down at Your presence,

[2]as when fire kindles brushwood,
as fire causes water to boil,

to make Your name known to Your adversaries,
that the nations might tremble at Your presence.

[3]When You did awesome things, which
we were not looking for,
You came down, and the mountains quaked at Your presence.

[4]And since ancient times, no one has heard,
none has given ear,
no eye has seen a God besides You,
who acts for those who wait for Him.

[5]You meet him who works righteousness
[and rejoiceth him that remembers][b] you in Your ways;

in [righteousness there] is an eternity,
and [such] will be saved.

a. Bracketed words in verse 17 are from JST.
b. Words in brackets in verse 5 are from JST.

6 But [we have sinned][a];
we have all become as one who is unclean,
and our righteous deeds like filthy garments,

and all of us wither like a leaf,
and our iniquities, like the wind, take us away.

7 [And none][b] calls on Your name,
who rouses Himself to take hold of You,

for You have hidden Your face from us
and delivered us into the hand of our iniquity.

8 But now, O LORD, You are our Father. We are the clay
and You are our potter; all of us are the work of Your hand.

9 O LORD, be not exceedingly angry,
nor remember iniquity forever.
Behold, look please, we are all Your people.

10 Your holy cities have become a wilderness.
Zion is a wilderness;
Jerusalem has become desolation.

11 Our holy and glorious House {Temple},
where our fathers praised You, has been burned by fire,
and all our pleasant places have become ruins.

12 At such things, O LORD, will You hold yourself back?
Will You keep silent and severely afflict us?

THE INIQUITY OF ANCIENT ISRAEL (65:1–7)

The LORD

65 1 "I [am found of them who seek after Me;
I give unto all of them that ask of Me][c];
I am [not] found of them that sought Me not,
[or that inquired not after Me:

I said unto My servant, "Behold Me,[d]
look upon Me,

I will send you] unto a nation that [are]not called by My name."

---

a. Words in brackets are from JST.
b. From JST.
c. Bracketed words in verses 1–2 are from JST.
d. *Here am I, here am I.* This expression can also be translated, "Behold me, behold me." Here am I is generally uttered by God's prophets, but here the Lord uses the expression.

2 [For] I have spread out My hands all day to a people,
who walk [not in My ways,
and their works are evil and] not good,
[and they walk] after their own thoughts.

3 The people who continually provoke Me to My face,
sacrificing in gardens
and burning incense upon bricks,

4 who sit in tombs
and spend the night in secret places,

who eat the flesh of pigs
and broth of abominable [beasts and pollute] their vessels.

5 Who say,

Wicked
'Keep to yourself; do not come near me,
for I am too holy for you.'

The Lord
These are smoke in My nostrils,
fire that burns all day.

6 Behold, it is written before Me,
"I will not remain silent,

but I will repay,
and I will repay into their bosom

7 both your iniquities
and your father's iniquities,"

Isaiah
says the Lord,

The Lord
"because they burned incense on the mountains
and taunted Me on the hills,

and I will measure their former deeds into their bosom."

Blessings for the Righteous, Cursings for the Sinful (65:8–16)

Isaiah
8 Thus the Lord says,

The Lord
"As the new wine is found in the cluster, and one says,

Unnamed individual
'Do not destroy it, for a blessing is in it,'

The Lord
so, I will do for My servants' sake and not destroy them all.

9 And I will bring forth offspring from Jacob
and from Judah, those who will inherit My mountains;

My chosen[a] will inherit it,
and My servants will dwell there.

[10]And Sharon will become a pasture for flocks,
and the Valley of Achor, a place for herds to lie down,

for My people
who have sought Me.

[11]But you who forsake the Lord,
who forget My holy mountain,

who set a table for Fortune
and fill a jug of mixed wine for Meni,

[12]I have destined you to the sword,
and all of you will bow down to the slaughter,

because I called, but you did not answer;
I spoke, but you did not listen,

but you did evil in My eyes,
and I did not delight in what you chose."

Isaiah [13]Therefore, thus says the Lord,

The Lord "Behold, My servants will eat,
but you will be hungry.

Behold, My servants will drink,
but you will be thirsty.

Behold, My servants will rejoice,
but you will be put to shame.

[14]Behold, My servants will sing with gladness of heart,
but you will cry out for pain of heart,

and you will wail for anguish of spirit.
[15]You will leave your name as a curse for My chosen ones,

and the Lord, the Lord, will slay you,
but He will call His servants a different name.

[16]So that he who invokes blessings in the land
will do so by the God of truth;

and he who takes an oath in the land
will take an oath by the God of truth,

---

a. "chosen" can also be translated "elect." God's chosen, His servants, are the righteous saints.

because the former troubles are forgotten
and are hidden from My eyes."

The Glorious Millennium (65:17–25)

The Lord 17 "For behold, I create new heavens
and a new earth,

and the former things will not be remembered,
nor come upon the heart.

18 But rejoice
and be joyful forever in that which I create,

for behold, I create Jerusalem for joy
and its people, for exultation.

19 I will be joyful in Jerusalem
and rejoice in My people,

and there will no more be heard in it the sound of weeping,
and the cry of distress.

20 [In those days][a] there will not be from
there an infant of days,
nor an old man who does not fill out his [day],

for the child will [not] die [but live to be] a hundred years old;
but the sinner [living to be] a hundred
years old, will be accursed.

21 They will build houses and inhabit them,
and they will plant vineyards and eat their fruit.

22 They will not build and another inhabit;
they will not plant, and another eat.

For the days of My people will be like the days of a tree,
and My chosen ones will long enjoy the work of their hands.

23 They will not labor in vain
or give birth for calamity,

for they are the offspring of the blessed of the Lord,
and their descendants with them.

24 And it will come to pass, before they call, I will answer;
while they are yet speaking, I will hear.

---

a. Bracketed words in verse 20 are from JST.

[25]The wolf and the lamb will feed together,
and the lion will eat straw like the ox,
and dust will be the food of the serpent;

they will not harm
nor destroy in all My holy mountain,"

Isaiah says the Lord.

The Apostasy of Ancient Israel and Their Punishment (66:1–6)

Isaiah **66** [1]Thus says the Lord,

The Lord "Heaven is My throne,
and the earth is My footstool.

Where is the House that you will build for Me?
And where is My resting place?

[2]My hand has made all these things,
and so, all these things exist,"

Isaiah declares the Lord.

The Lord "And to this one I look—
to the humble and the contrite in spirit,
who trembles at My word.

[3]Whoever slaughters an ox
is like one who smites a man;

whoever sacrifices a lamb
is like one who breaks a dog's neck;

whoever presents a cereal offering
is like one who offers swine's blood;

whoever makes a memorial offering of frankincense
is like one who blesses an idol.

These have chosen their own ways,
and in their abominations their soul delights.

[4]I also will choose affliction for them,

and I will bring upon them what they dread,

because when I called, no one answered;
I spoke, but they did not listen;

they did what was evil in My eyes,
and they chose that in which I do not delight."

Isaiah	5 Hear the word of the LORD, you who tremble at His word:
The LORD	"Your brothers who hate you and cast you out for My name's sake have said,"
Haters	"Let the LORD be glorified that we may see your rejoicing."
The LORD	"But they will be put to shame."
Isaiah	6 The sound of a roar in the city, a voice from the Temple, the sound of the LORD dealing punishment to His enemies.

LADY ZION AND HER CHILDREN IN THE LAST DAYS (66:7–13)

Isaiah	7 Before she {Zion} was in labor, she gave birth; before her labor pang came upon her, she delivered a son. 8 Who has heard such a thing? Who has seen such things? Is the land born in one day, a nation brought forth in one moment? For Zion was in labor; she also brought forth her children.
The LORD	9 "Will I who bring on labor not bring forth birth?"
Isaiah	says the LORD.
The LORD	"Will I who cause birth to shut the womb?"
Isaiah	says your God.
The LORD	10 "Rejoice with Jerusalem, and all who love her be joyful for her; exult with her with exultation, all who mourn over her, 11 that you may nurse and be satisfied with her comforting breast, that you may drink deeply with delight from her glorious abundance."[a]
Isaiah	12 For thus says the LORD,

a. The Hebrew *ziz*, translated "abundance," also means "breast." It is a synonym for "breast" in the previous line.

The LORD "Behold, I will extend peace to her like a river,
and the glory of the nations like an overflowing stream,

and you will be nursed and be carried on her side,
and you will be bounced on her knees.

13 As one whom his mother comforts, so I will comfort you;
you will be comforted in Jerusalem.

And you will see, and your heart will exult,
and your bones will flourish like the grass."

THE LORD WILL RETURN IN GREAT POWER (66:14B–18A)

Isaiah 14 The hand of the LORD will be known to His servants,
but His indignation against His enemies.

15 For behold, the LORD will come with fire,
His chariots like a whirlwind,

to render His anger with fury
and His rebuke with flames of fire.

16 For with fire and by His sword the LORD
will execute judgment on all flesh,
and those pierced by the LORD will be many.

The LORD 17 "Those who sanctify themselves
and purify themselves in the gardens,

behind one in the center,
eating pig's flesh and abominable things and the mouse,

they will come to an end together,"

Isaiah declares the LORD.

The LORD 18 "For I know their works
and their thoughts."

GATHERING FROM ALL NATIONS (66:18B–21)

The LORD 18 "{The time} is coming to gather all nations
and tongues.

And they will come,
and they will see My glory.

[19]And I will set a token among them,[a]
and from them I will send survivors to the nations,

to Tarshish, Pul, and Lud, who draw the bow,
to Tubal, Javan, to the distant islands

that have not heard My fame or seen My glory;
and they will declare My glory among the nations.

[20]And they will bring all your brothers from all nations,
as an offering to the Lord, on horses, and in chariots,
and in covered wagons, and upon mules, and upon
dromedaries, to My holy mountain in Jerusalem,"

Isaiah says the Lord,

The Lord "just as the children of Israel bring the offering in a pure vessel to the House of the Lord. [21]And some of them I will also take for priests and for Levites,"

Isaiah says the Lord.

The Righteous's Offspring and Name Will Remain (66:22–24)

The Lord [22]"For as the new heavens and the new earth,
which I make, will remain before Me,"

Isaiah declares the Lord,

The Lord "so, your offspring
and your name will remain.

[23]And it will come to pass, from new moon[b] to new moon,
and from Sabbath to Sabbath, all flesh
will come to worship before Me,"

Isaiah says the Lord.

The Lord [24]"And they will go forth and look on the dead bodies of the men who have rebelled against Me, for their worm will not die, their fire will not be quenched, and they will be an abhorrence to all flesh."

---

a. The Hebrew word *'ot* may be translated "token," like the one that the Lord gave to Moses (Exodus 3:12); or "sign," like that offered to king Ahaz (7:11).

b. "New moon" (Hebrew, *chodesh*) can also be translated "month."

Appendix

Representative List of Chiasms in the Book of Isaiah

The following list presents about 130 examples of chiasmus in Isaiah. Note that many chiastic structures in the Hebrew language are not always evident when translated into English. This is partly due to the different sentence structures in the two languages. Many of the following examples of chiasmus are followed with the word *Hebrew* in parentheses, indicating that the chiasmus exists in the Hebrew but has lost its chiastic value in the English translation.

Isaiah 1:11

A I have eaten
 B rams, fatted steers
 B' bulls, lambs, male goats
A' I do not desire

Isaiah 1:21

A prostitute
 B justice
 B' righteousness
A' murderers

Isaiah 1:21–26

A faithful town
 B justice ... righteousness
  C silver ... dross
   D rulers ... thieves
    E the Lord of Hosts
    E' the mighty One of Israel
   D' adversaries ... enemies
  C' dross ... slag
 B' judges ... counselors
A' faithful town

Isaiah 2:3

A from Zion
 B law
 B' word of the Lord
A' from Jerusalem

Isaiah 2:3–5

A house of the God of Jacob ... we may walk
 B nations
  C swords into plowshares
  C' spears into pruninghooks
 B' nation ... nation
A' house of Jacob ... let us walk

Isaiah 3:1–8

A Jerusalem ... Judah
 B bread
  C judge ... prophet ... captain
   D young people
    E everyone by another
    E' everyone by a neighbor
   D' young person
  C' you will be our leader
 B' bread
A' Jerusalem ... Judah

Isaiah 3:8 (Hebrew)

A has stumbled
B Jerusalem
B' Judah
A' has fallen

Isaiah 5:7

A vineyard
B house of Israel
B' men of Judah
A' delightful plant

Isaiah 5:11–13

A strong drink ... wine
B banquets
C deeds of the Lord
C' work of His hands
B' hungry
A' thirst

Isaiah 5:14–17

A opened its mouth
B bow down ... humbled
C exalted
B' shows Himself holy
A' feed ... feed

Isaiah 5:20

A evil
B good
B' good
A' evil

Isaiah 5:20

A darkness
B light
B' light
A' darkness

Isaiah 5:20

A bitter
B sweet
B' sweet
A' bitter

Isaiah 5:21

A wise
B in their own eyes
B' in their own sight
A' understanding

Isaiah 6:7

A is removed
B your iniquity
B' your sin
A' atoned

Isaiah 6:10

A heart
B ears
C eyes
C' eyes
B' ears
A' hearts

Isaiah 7:7–9

A it will not happen
B head ... head
C Ephraim will be shattered
C' it is no longer a people
B' head ... head
A' will not hold firm

Isaiah 7:22

A eat
B butter
B' butter
A' eat

Isaiah 9:21

A Manasseh
B Ephraim
B' Ephraim
A' Manasseh

Isaiah 10:4 (Hebrew)

A crouch
B under the prisoner

B' under the slain
A' fall

Isaiah 10:6

A I will send him
B against a godless nation
B' against the people of my wrath
A' will I command him

Isaiah 10:20–21

A remnant of Israel
B survivors of the house of Jacob
C rely upon him who smote them
C' rely upon the Lord
B' remnant will return
A' remnant of Jacob

Isaiah 10:24

A Assyria
B smite you with a rod
B' lift his staff
A' Egypt

Isaiah 11:1 (Hebrew)

A will come forth
B rod
B' branch
A' will grow

Isaiah 11:4

A smite the earth
B rod of his mouth
B' breath of his lips
A' slay the wicked

Isaiah 11:6 (Hebrew)

A will dwell
B wolf ... with the lamb
B' leopard ... with the kid
A' will lie down

Isaiah 11:8 (Hebrew)

A will play
B nursing babe ... on the hole of the viper
B' toddler ... on the hole of the viper
A' will put his hand

Isaiah 11:13

A Ephraim
B Judah
B' Judah
A' Ephraim

Isaiah 13:10 (Hebrew)

A will be darkened
B sun
B' moon
A' will not cause its light to shine

Isaiah 13:16

A plundered
B their houses
B' their wives
A' ravished

Isaiah 13:21 (Hebrew)

A will dwell there
B owls
B' wild goats
A' will leap about there

Isaiah 14:15

A Sheol
B brought down
B' to the depths
A' pit

Isaiah 14:25 (Hebrew)

A be removed
B his yoke
B' his burden
A' be removed

Isaiah 14:25

A to break the Assyrian
B My land
B' My mountains
A' I will trample him

Isaiah 14:30 (Hebrew)

A shall feed
  B poor
  B' needy
A' lie down in safety

Isaiah 14:30

A I will kill
  B your root
  B' your remnant
A' it shall slay

Isaiah 16:7–12

A Moab
  B Kir-hareseth
  C Heshbon
    D Sibmah
      E Jazer
      E' Jazer
    D' Sibmah
  C' Heshbon
  B' Kir-hareseth
A' Moab

Isaiah 17:10

A you have forgotten
  B *God of Your Salvation*
  B' *Rock of Your Stronghold*
A' you have not remembered

Isaiah 18:6 (Hebrew)

A will summer upon them
  B birds of prey
  B' wild animals
A' will winter upon them

Isaiah 19:21

A Lord
  B be known
    C Egyptians
    C' Egyptians
  B' know
A' Lord

Isaiah 21:12

A you
  B inquire
  B' inquire
A' you

Isaiah 22:19

A I will thrust you
  B from your station
  B' from your position
A' he will cast you

Isaiah 22:22

A open
  B shut
  B' shut
A' open

Isaiah 25:10–11

A hand of the Lord
  B trodden down
  B' trodden down
A' his hands

Isaiah 26:7

A righteous
  B level
  B' level
A' righteous

Isaiah 26:9–10 (Hebrew)

A righteousness
  B learn
    C inhabitants of the world
    C' wicked
  B' learn
A' righteousness

Isaiah 26:19 (Hebrew)

A will live
  B dead men
  B' bodies
A' will ... arise

Isaiah 27:5 (Hebrew)

A he will make
  B peace
  B' peace
A' he will make

Isaiah 27:11 (Hebrew)

A will not have compassion
  B their Maker
  B' their Fashioner
A' will show them no favor

Isaiah 28:12

A to those whom He has said
  B this is the rest
    C give rest to the weary
  B' this is the resting place
A' they are not willing to hear

Isaiah 28:15–18

A covenant with death ...
Sheol, we made an agreement ...
overflowing scourge
  B lie our place of refuge ... shelter
    C laying a stone
      D precious cornerstone
      D' sure foundation
    C' measuring line ... plumb line
  B' refuge of lies ... shelter
A' covenant with death ...
agreement with Sheol ...
overflowing scourge

Isaiah 29:10

A shut your eyes
  B prophets
    C your rulers
  B' seers
A' He has covered

Isaiah 29:14 (Hebrew)

A shall perish
  B wisdom of their wise
  B' understanding of their prudent
A' will be hid

Isaiah 29:17 (Hebrew)

A will be turned
  B Lebanon
    C fertile field
    C' fertile field
  B' forest
A' be regarded

Isaiah 30:8 (Hebrew)

A write it
  B tablet
  B' book
A' inscribe it

Isaiah 30:22 (Hebrew)

A you will defile
  B idols, overlaid with silver
  B' gold-plated molten images
A' you will cast them away

Isaiah 32:1 (Hebrew)

A will reign
  B king
  B' princes
A' will govern

Isaiah 32:3 (Hebrew)

A will not be closed
  B eyes of those who see
  B' ears of those who hear
A' will listen

Isaiah 32:6 (Hebrew)

A folly
  B speaks
  B' works
A' iniquity

Isaiah 32:6 (Hebrew)

A to make empty
  B the hungry
  B' the thirsty
A' to deprive

Isaiah 32:16

A reside
  B in the wilderness
    C justice
    C' righteousness
  B' in the fruitful field
A' will dwell (32:16)

Isaiah 33:14

A sinners in Zion
  B are afraid
  B' trembling seizes
A' the godless

Isaiah 33:17 (Hebrew)

A King
  B your eyes will see
  B' they will see
A' land

Isaiah 34:4

A host
  B heaven
  B' heavens
A' host

Isaiah 34:5–8

A Edom
  B judgment
    C fat
      D lambs and goats
        E sacrifice
        E' slaughter
      D' bulls ... mighty ones
    C' fat
  B' vengeance
A' Zion

Isaiah 35:1–2

A be joyful
  B blossom
  B' blossom
A' be joyful

Isaiah 35:10

A everlasting joy
  B upon their heads
  B' they will obtain
A' exultation and rejoicing

Isaiah 36:18–19

A deliver ... hand
  B where are the gods
  B' where are the gods
A' delivered ... hand

Isaiah 38:12

A My dwelling
  B is pulled up
  B' is removed from me
A' like a tent of a shepherd

Isaiah 40:12 (Hebrew)

A measured
  B hollow of His hand
    C waters
    C' heavens
  B' width
A' marked off

Isaiah 40:14

A made Him understand
  B taught him
  B' taught him
A' made Him know the way of understanding

Isaiah 40:26 (Hebrew)

A Lift up ... on high
  B your eyes
  B' see
A' who created these

Isaiah 40:26

A calling them all by name
  B abundant might
  B' mighty power
A' not one is missing

Isaiah 40:27 (Hebrew)

A is hidden
  B my way
    C from the Lord
    C' my God
  B' my judgment
A' is passed over

Isaiah 40:28–31

A does not faint
  B is not weary
    C He gives power to the faint
      D strength
        E youth
        E' young men
      D' strength
    C' they will go up with wings like eagles
  B' not grow weary
A' not faint

Isaiah 41:4

A I the Lord
  B first
  B' last ones
A' I am He

Isaiah 42:12

A let them give glory
  B the Lord
  B' his praise
A' declare

Isaiah 42:15 (Hebrew)

A lay waste
  B mountains and hills
  B' all their vegetation
A' dry up

Isaiah 43:1–21

A your Fashioner
  B waters ... rivers
    C fire ... scorched
      D Lord, God, Holy One, Savior
        E Egypt, Cush, Seba
          F I give, I will bring, gather, say, created, fashioned
            G you are My witnesses
              H I am the Lord
              H' there is no Savior besides Me
            G' you are My witnesses
          F' I act
        E' Babylon, Chaldeans
      D' Lord, Holy One, Creator, King
    C' snuffed like a wick
  B' water ... rivers
A' I have fashioned this people

Isaiah 43:18

A do not remember
  B former things
  B' things of old
A' nor consider

Isaiah 43:19–20

A wilderness and desert
  B beast
  B' jackals and ostriches
A' wilderness and desert

Isaiah 44:21

A Israel
  B My servant
  B' My servant
A' Israel

Isaiah 45:1 (Hebrew)

A before him
  B I will loose
  B' to open
A' before him

Isaiah 45:22–25

A ends of the earth
  B God
    C righteousness
      D every knee
      D' every tongue
    C' righteousness
  B' Lord
A' seed of Israel

Isaiah 48:1

A are called
  B Israel
  B' Judah
A' came forth

Isaiah 48:1

A who swear
  B by the name of the Lord
  B' the God of Israel
A' acknowledge

Isaiah 48:3, 5

A announced
  B the former things
  B' of old
A' told

Isaiah 48:4 (Hebrew)

A iron
  B neck
  B' forehead
A' brass

Isaiah 48:18 (Hebrew)

A like a river
  B your peace
  B' your righteousness
A' like the waves of the sea

Isaiah 48:21

A waters
  B rock
  B' rock
A' water

Isaiah 49:1

A O you house of Israel
  B all you that are broken off and are driven out
    C because of the wickedness of the pastors of My people
  B' all you that are broken off, that are scattered abroad
A' O house of Israel

Isaiah 49:1

A Lord has called me
  B from the womb
  B' from my mother's belly
A' he assigned my name

Isaiah 49:1–6

A islands
  B peoples
    C womb
      D made me a sharpened arrow
        E You are my servant
        E' I have labored
      D' my reward is with my God
    C' womb
  B' tribes of Jacob
A' ends of the earth

Isaiah 49:11

A And I will make all My mountains
  B a way

B' and My highways
A' will be exalted

Isaiah 49:13 (Hebrew)

A has comforted
B His people
B' His afflicted
A' will have compassion

Isaiah 49:14 (Hebrew)

A has forsaken me
B Lord
B' Lord
A' has forgotten me

Isaiah 49:18 (Hebrew)

A as with an ornament
B you will surely clothe all of them
B' bind them on
A' as a bride

Isaiah 49:22 (Hebrew)

A I will lift up
B nations
B' peoples
A' raise up

Isaiah 49:22 (Hebrew)

A they shall bring
B sons in their lap
B' daughters ... upon their shoulders
A' will be carried

Isaiah 49:24–25

A prey
B captives
B' captives
A' prey

Isaiah 50:1

A thus says the Lord
B Have I put you away
B' have I cast you off forever
A' thus says the Lord

Isaiah 50:1 (Hebrew)

A your mother
B put you away
C sold
C' sold
B' put you away
A' your mother

Isaiah 50:3

A clothe
B blackness
B' sackcloth
A' covering

Isaiah 50:4

A he wakens
B morning
B' morning
A' he wakens

Isaiah 51:4 (Hebrew)

A hearken
B to me
C My people
C' My nation
B' to me
A' give ear

Isaiah 51:7 (Hebrew)

A fear not
B insults of men
B' their revilings
A' neither be dismayed

Isaiah 51:11

A will overtake them
B gladness and joy
B' sorrow and sighing
A' will flee away

Isaiah 51:15

A I am the Lord your God
B who stirs up the sea
B' and its waves roar
A' the Lord of Hosts is His name

Isaiah 51:23

A pass over
B like the ground
B' like the street
A' passed over

Isaiah 53:7

A He opened not His mouth
B as a lamb
B' as an ewe lamb
A' He openeth not his mouth

Isaiah 54:2 (Hebrew)

A enlarge
B the place of your tent
B' the curtains of your habitations
A' stretched out

Isaiah 54:2 (Hebrew)

A lengthen
B your cords
B' your stakes
A' strengthen

Isaiah 54:13

A your children
B taught of the Lord
B' peace
A' your children

Isaiah 55:8–9

A My thoughts
B your thoughts
C your ways
D My ways
E heavens are higher
E' than the earth
D' My ways
C' your ways
B' My thoughts
A' your thoughts

Isaiah 56:5 (Hebrew)

A I will give
B name
B' name
A' I will give

Isaiah 56:9

A beasts of the field
B come to eat
A' beasts in the forest

Isaiah 57:15

A contrite
B lowly in spirit
B' lowly in spirit
A' contrite

Isaiah 57:20–21

A the wicked
B tossing sea
C it cannot be quiet
C' its waters toss up mire and dirt
B' no peace
A' the wicked

Isaiah 58:10 (Hebrew)

A pour out
B hungry
C soul
C' soul
B' afflicted
A' satisfy

Isaiah 59:3 (Hebrew)

A have spoken
B lies
B' wickedness
A' mutters

Isaiah 59:16–17

A salvation
  B righteousness
  B' righteousness
A' salvation

Isaiah 60:1–3 (Hebrew)

A Arise,
  B shine;
    C for your light has come,
      D and the glory
        E of the Lord
          F has risen upon you.
            G For behold, the darkness will cover the earth,
            G' and gross darkness the people:
          F' will arise on you,
        E' but the Lord
      D' and His glory will appear on you.
    C' And the nations will go to your light
  B' and kings to the brightness
A' of your rising.

Isaiah 60:13 (Hebrew)

A to beautify
  B the place of My sanctuary
  B' the place of My feet
A' make ... glorious

Isaiah 60:16 (Hebrew)

A you will suck
  B the milk of nations
  B' the breast of kings
A' you will suck

Isaiah 62:1 (Hebrew)

A as brightness
  B her righteousness
  B' her salvation
A' as burning torch

Isaiah 63:16

A You are our Father
  B Abraham does not know us
  B' Israel does not acknowledge us
A' You, O Lord, are our Father

Isaiah 65:18

A be joyful forever
  B I create
  B' I create
A' for joy ... for exultation

www.ingramcontent.com/pod-product-compliance
Ingram Content Group UK Ltd.
Pitfield, Milton Keynes, MK11 3LW, UK
UKHW020424250726
13967UKWH00007B/2804

9 781971 818009